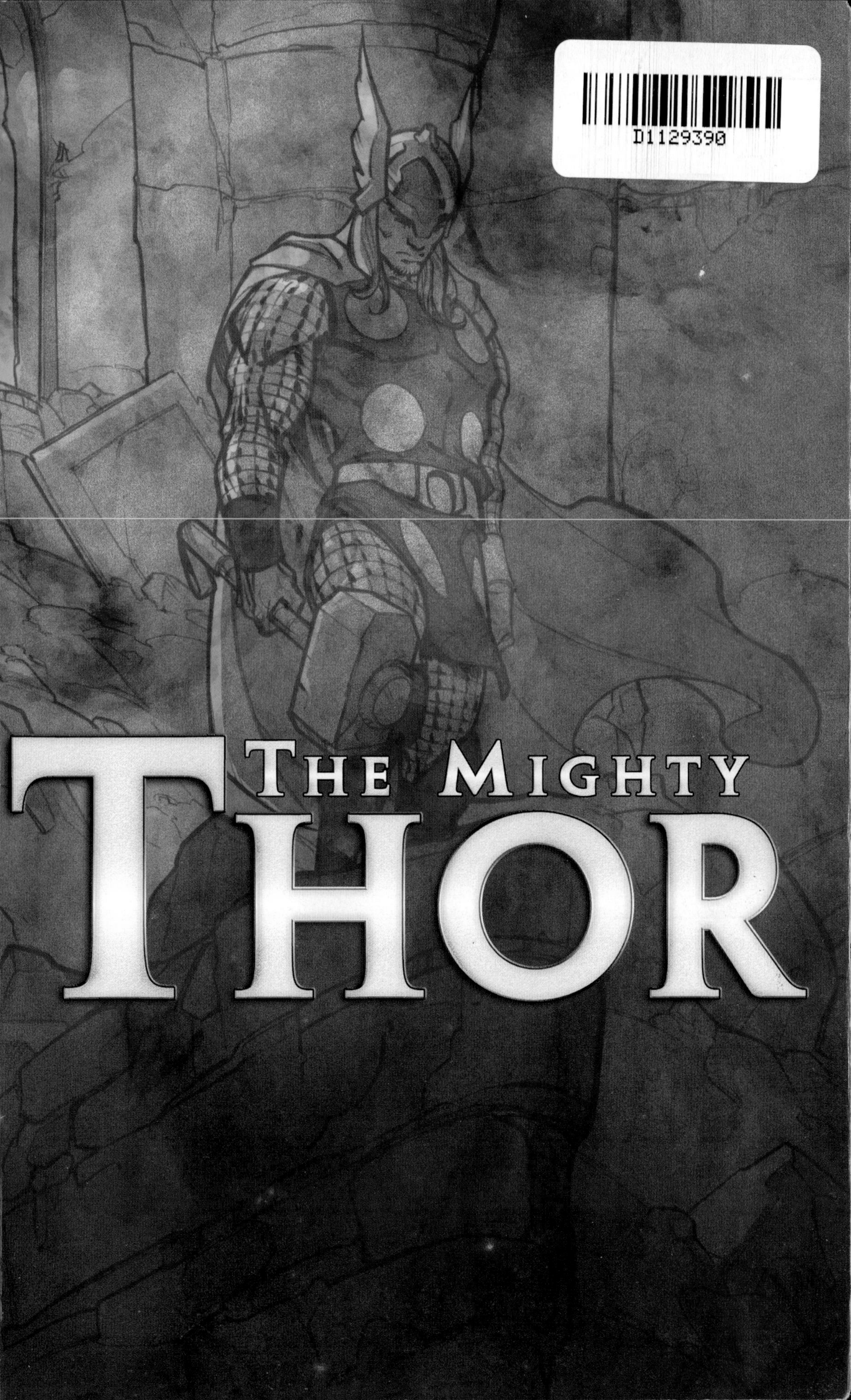
THE MIGHTY
THOR

COLLECTION EDITOR: JENNIFER GRÜNWALD · ASSISTANT EDITORS: ALEX STARBUCK & NELSON RIBEIRO
EDITOR, SPECIAL PROJECTS: MARK D. BEAZLEY · SENIOR EDITOR, SPECIAL PROJECTS: JEFF YOUNGQUIST
SENIOR VICE PRESIDENT OF SALES: DAVID GABRIEL
SVP OF BRAND PLANNING & COMMUNICATIONS: MICHAEL PASCIULLO

EDITOR IN CHIEF: AXEL ALONSO · CHIEF CREATIVE OFFICER: JOE QUESADA
PUBLISHER: DAN BUCKLEY · EXECUTIVE PRODUCER: ALAN FINE

THE MIGHTY THOR BY MATT FRACTION VOL. 3. Contains material originally published in magazine form as THE MIGHTY THOR #12.1 and #13-17. First printing 2012. Hardcover ISBN# 978-0-7851-6166-0. Softcover ISBN
978-0-7851-6167-7. Published by MARVEL WORLDWIDE, INC., a subsidiary of MARVEL ENTERTAINMENT, LLC. OFFICE OF PUBLICATION: 135 West 50th Street, New York, NY 10020. Copyright © 2012 Marvel Characters, Inc.
All rights reserved. Hardcover: $24.99 per copy in the U.S. and $27.99 in Canada (GST #R127032852). Softcover: $19.99 per copy in the U.S. and $21.99 in Canada (GST #R127032852). Canadian Agreement #40668537.
All characters featured in this issue and the distinctive names and likenesses thereof, and all related indicia are trademarks of Marvel Characters, Inc. No similarity between any of the names, characters, persons, and/or
institutions in this magazine with those of any living or dead person or institution is intended, and any such similarity which may exist is purely coincidental. **Printed in the U.S.A.** ALAN FINE, EVP - Office of the President, Marvel
Worldwide, Inc. and EVP & CMO Marvel Characters B.V.; DAN BUCKLEY, Publisher & President - Print, Animation & Digital Divisions; JOE QUESADA, Chief Creative Officer; TOM BREVOORT, SVP of Publishing; DAVID BOGART, SVP
of Operations & Procurement, Publishing; RUWAN JAYATILLEKE, SVP & Associate Publisher, Publishing; C.B. CEBULSKI, SVP of Creator & Content Development; DAVID GABRIEL, SVP of Publishing Sales & Circulation; MICHAEL
PASCIULLO, SVP of Brand Planning & Communications; JIM O'KEEFE, VP of Operations & Logistics; DAN CARR, Executive Director of Publishing Technology; SUSAN CRESPI, Editorial Operations Manager; ALEX MORALES,
Publishing Operations Manager; STAN LEE, Chairman Emeritus. For information regarding advertising in Marvel Comics or on Marvel.com, please contact Niza Disla, Director of Marvel Partnerships, at ndisla@marvel.com.
For Marvel subscription inquiries, please call 800-217-9158. **Manufactured between 7/30/2012 and 9/10/2012 (hardcover), and 7/30/2012 and 3/11/2013 (softcover), by R.R. DONNELLEY, INC., SALEM, VA, USA.**

10 9 8 7 6 5 4 3 2 1

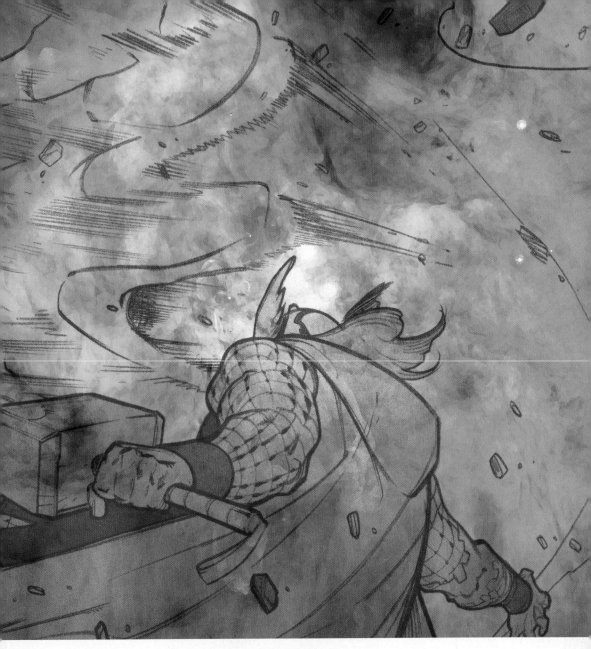

WRITER
MATT FRACTION

ARTISTS
BARRY KITSON WITH **JAY LEISTEN** (#12.1)
& **PEPE LARRAZ** (#13-17)

COLOR ARTISTS
FRANK D'ARMATA (#12.1-16) & **WIL QUINTANA** (#17)

LETTERER
VC'S JOE SABINO

COVER ART
OLIVIER COIPEL WITH **LAURA MARTIN** (#12.1)
AND **WALTER SIMONSON** WITH **PAUL MOUNTS** & **LAURA MARTIN** (#13-17)

ASSISTANT EDITOR
JOHN DENNING

EDITOR
LAUREN SANKOVITCH

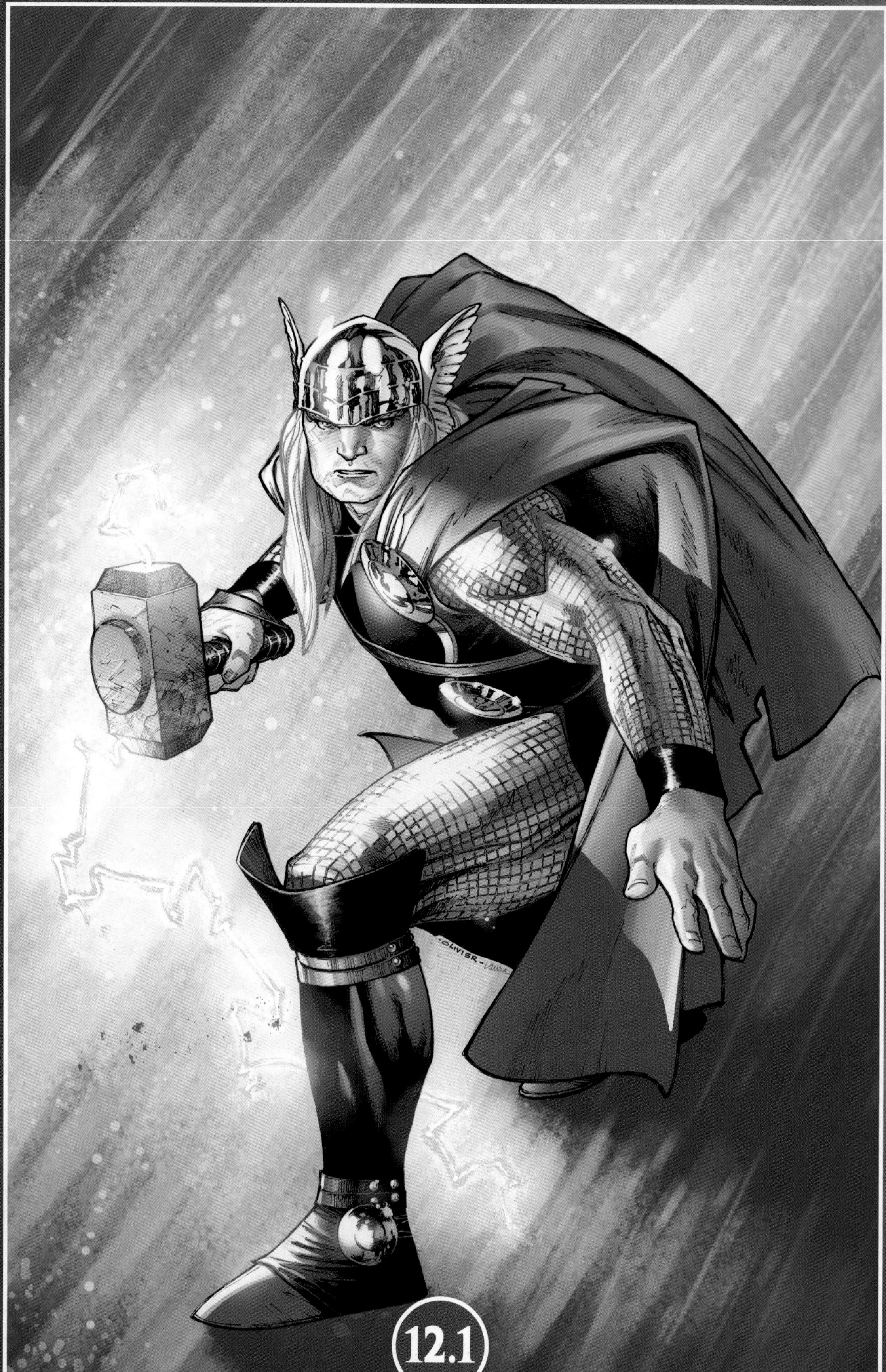
12.1

He is the son of Asgard, a golden city floating high above the Earth's surface, the capital of a new republic of Nine Worlds led by the All-Mother. He is the God of Thunder. He is an Avenger. He is—

The Mighty
THOR

THOR

SIF

VOLSTAGG

LOKI

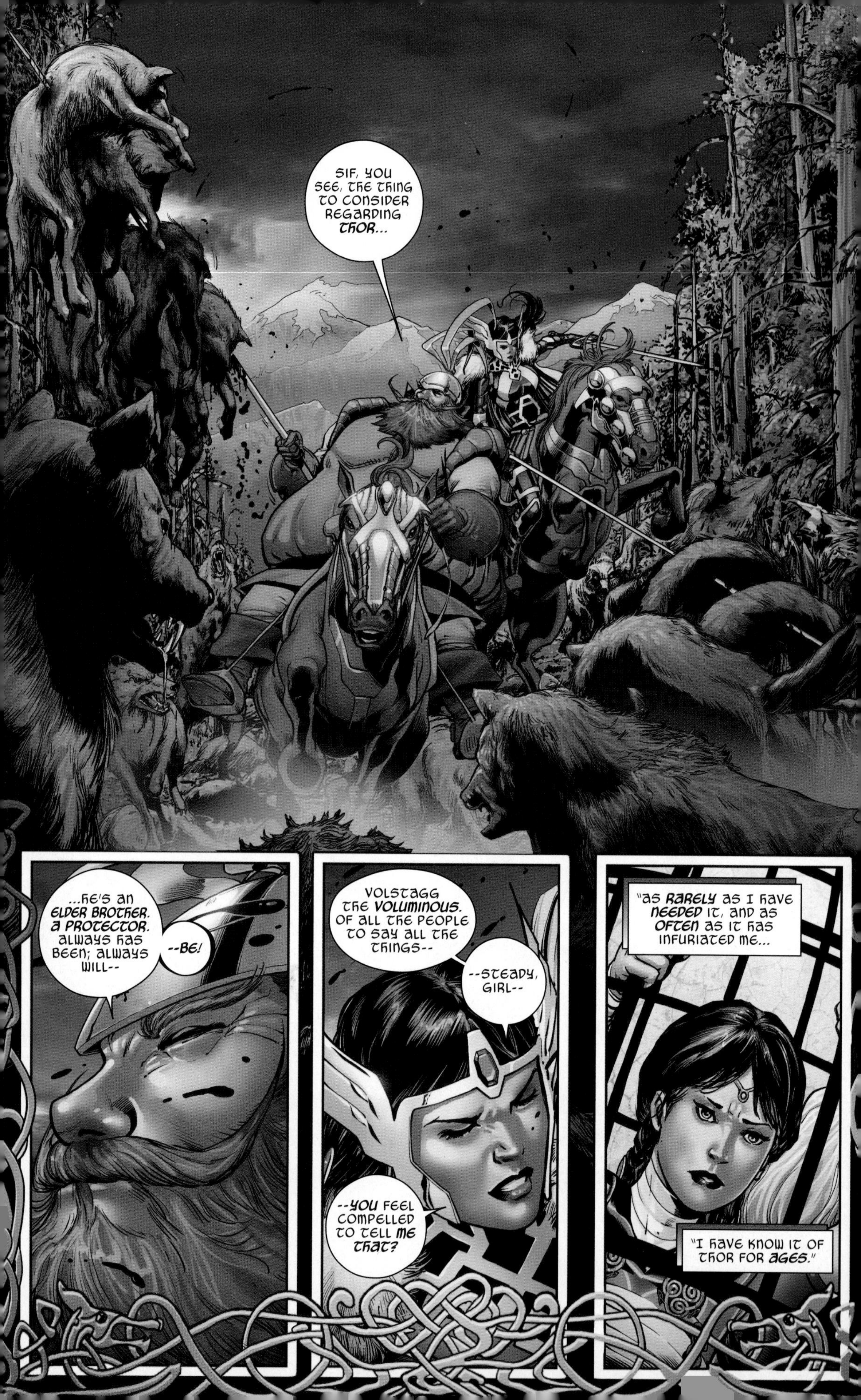

SIF, YOU SEE, THE THING TO CONSIDER REGARDING THOR...
...HE'S AN ELDER BROTHER. A PROTECTOR. ALWAYS HAS BEEN; ALWAYS WILL--
--BE!
VOLSTAGG THE VOLUMINOUS. OF ALL THE PEOPLE TO SAY ALL THE THINGS--
--STEADY, GIRL--
--YOU FEEL COMPELLED TO TELL ME THAT?
"AS RARELY AS I HAVE NEEDED IT, AND AS OFTEN AS IT HAS INFURIATED ME...
"I HAVE KNOW IT OF THOR FOR AGES."

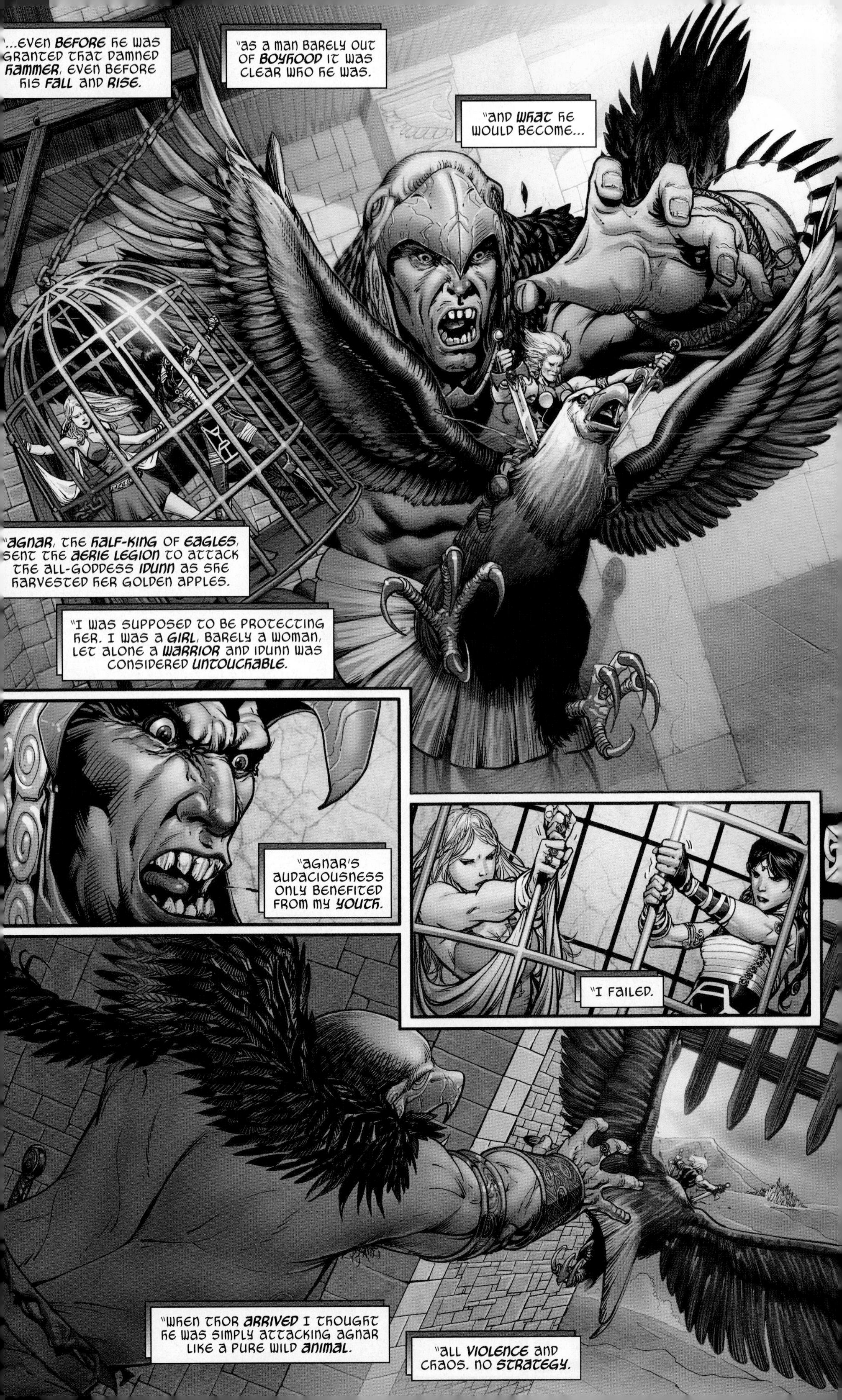
"...EVEN BEFORE HE WAS GRANTED THAT DAMNED HAMMER, EVEN BEFORE HIS FALL AND RISE.
"AS A MAN BARELY OUT OF BOYHOOD IT WAS CLEAR WHO HE WAS.
"AND WHAT HE WOULD BECOME...
"AGNAR, THE HALF-KING OF EAGLES, SENT THE AERIE LEGION TO ATTACK THE ALL-GODDESS IDUNN AS SHE HARVESTED HER GOLDEN APPLES.
"I WAS SUPPOSED TO BE PROTECTING HER. I WAS A GIRL, BARELY A WOMAN, LET ALONE A WARRIOR AND IDUNN WAS CONSIDERED UNTOUCHABLE.
"AGNAR'S AUDACIOUSNESS ONLY BENEFITED FROM MY YOUTH.
"I FAILED.
"WHEN THOR ARRIVED I THOUGHT HE WAS SIMPLY ATTACKING AGNAR LIKE A PURE WILD ANIMAL.
"ALL VIOLENCE AND CHAOS. NO STRATEGY.

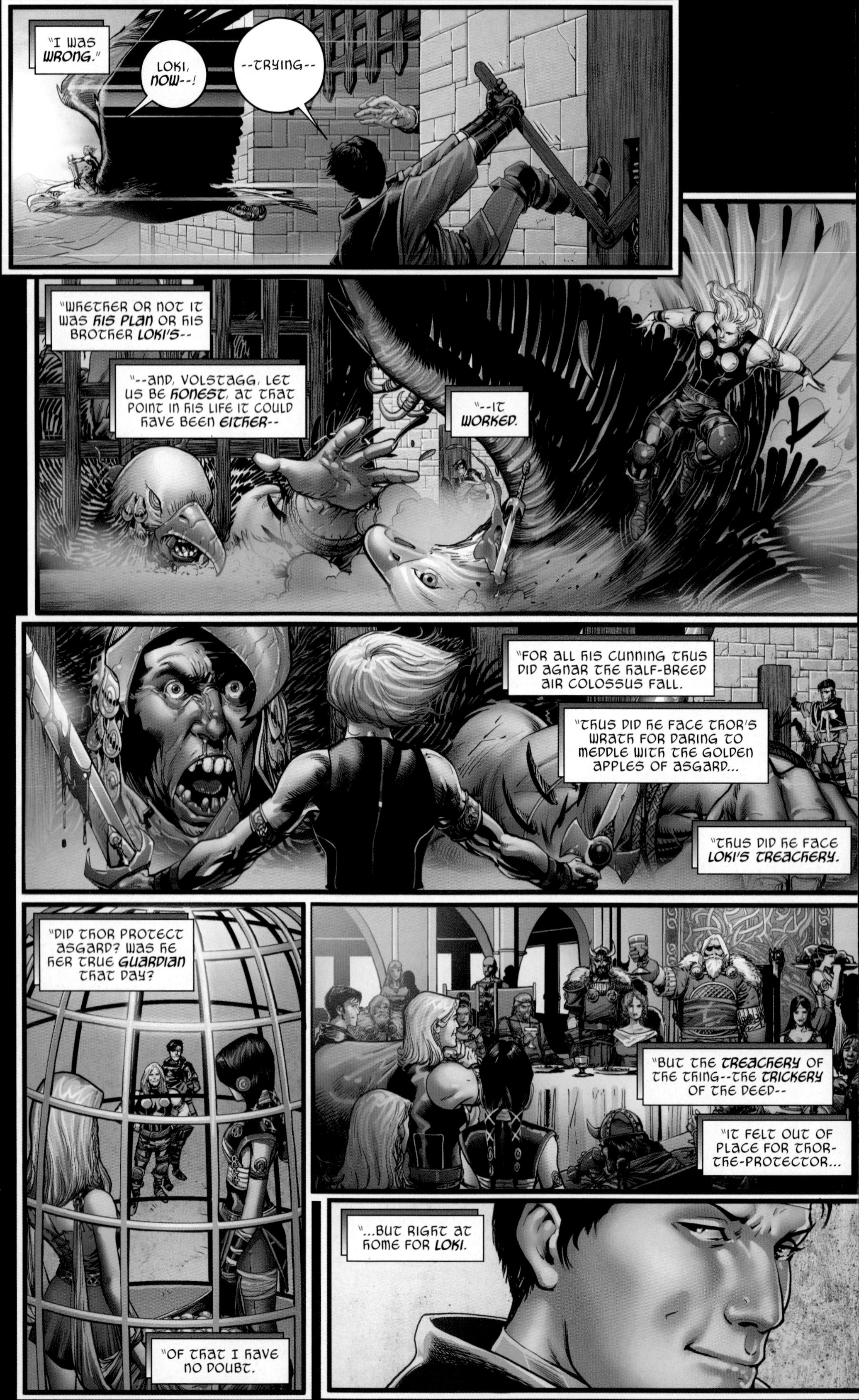
"I WAS WRONG."
LOKI, NOW--!
--TRYING--
"WHETHER OR NOT IT WAS HIS PLAN OR HIS BROTHER LOKI'S--
"--AND, VOLSTAGG, LET US BE HONEST, AT THAT POINT IN HIS LIFE IT COULD HAVE BEEN EITHER--
"--IT WORKED.
"FOR ALL HIS CUNNING THUS DID AGNAR THE HALF-BREED AIR COLOSSUS FALL.
"THUS DID HE FACE THOR'S WRATH FOR DARING TO MEDDLE WITH THE GOLDEN APPLES OF ASGARD...
"THUS DID HE FACE LOKI'S TREACHERY.
"DID THOR PROTECT ASGARD? WAS HE HER TRUE GUARDIAN THAT DAY?
"OF THAT I HAVE NO DOUBT.
"BUT THE TREACHERY OF THE THING--THE TRICKERY OF THE DEED--
"IT FELT OUT OF PLACE FOR THOR-THE-PROTECTOR...
"...BUT RIGHT AT HOME FOR LOKI.

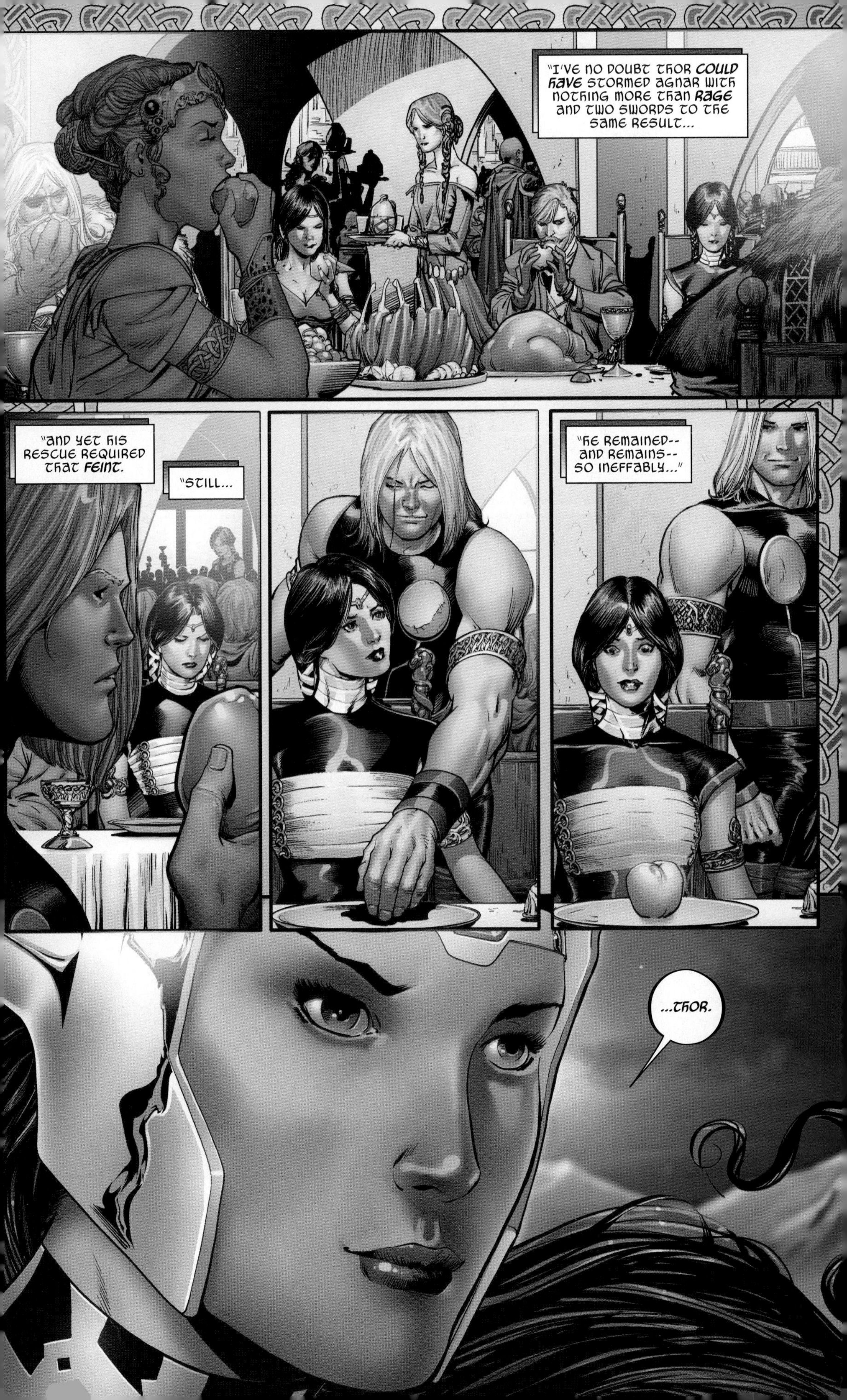
"I'VE NO DOUBT THOR COULD HAVE STORMED AGNAR WITH NOTHING MORE THAN RAGE AND TWO SWORDS TO THE SAME RESULT...
"AND YET HIS RESCUE REQUIRED THAT FEINT.
"STILL...
"HE REMAINED-- AND REMAINS-- SO INEFFABLY..."
...THOR.

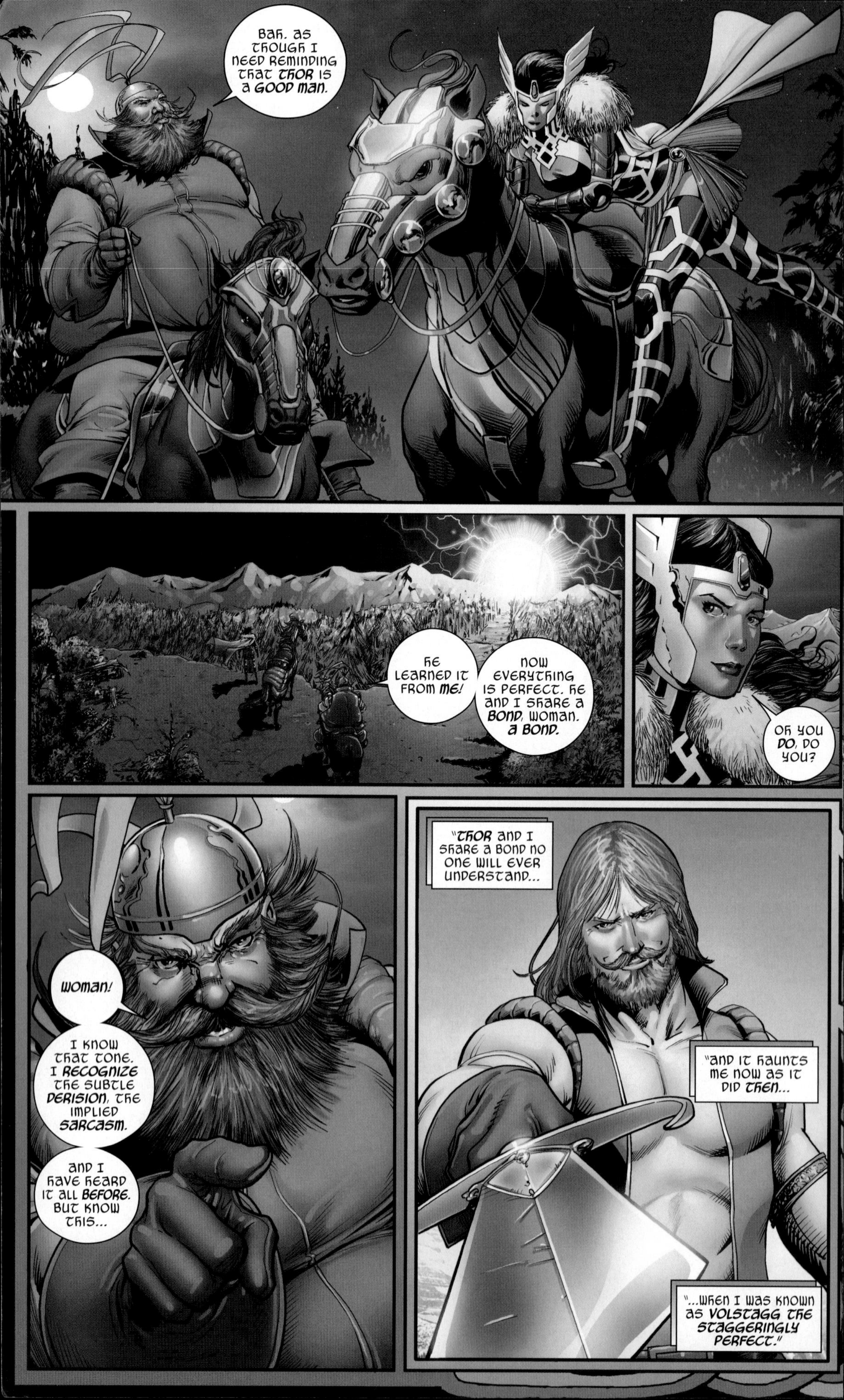
BAH. AS THOUGH I NEED REMINDING THAT THOR IS A GOOD MAN.
HE LEARNED IT FROM ME!
NOW EVERYTHING IS PERFECT. HE AND I SHARE A BOND, WOMAN. A BOND.
OH YOU DO, DO YOU?
WOMAN!
I KNOW THAT TONE. I RECOGNIZE THE SUBTLE DERISION, THE IMPLIED SARCASM.
AND I HAVE HEARD IT ALL BEFORE. BUT KNOW THIS...
"THOR AND I SHARE A BOND NO ONE WILL EVER UNDERSTAND...
"AND IT HAUNTS ME NOW AS IT DID THEN...
"...WHEN I WAS KNOWN AS VOLSTAGG THE STAGGERINGLY PERFECT."

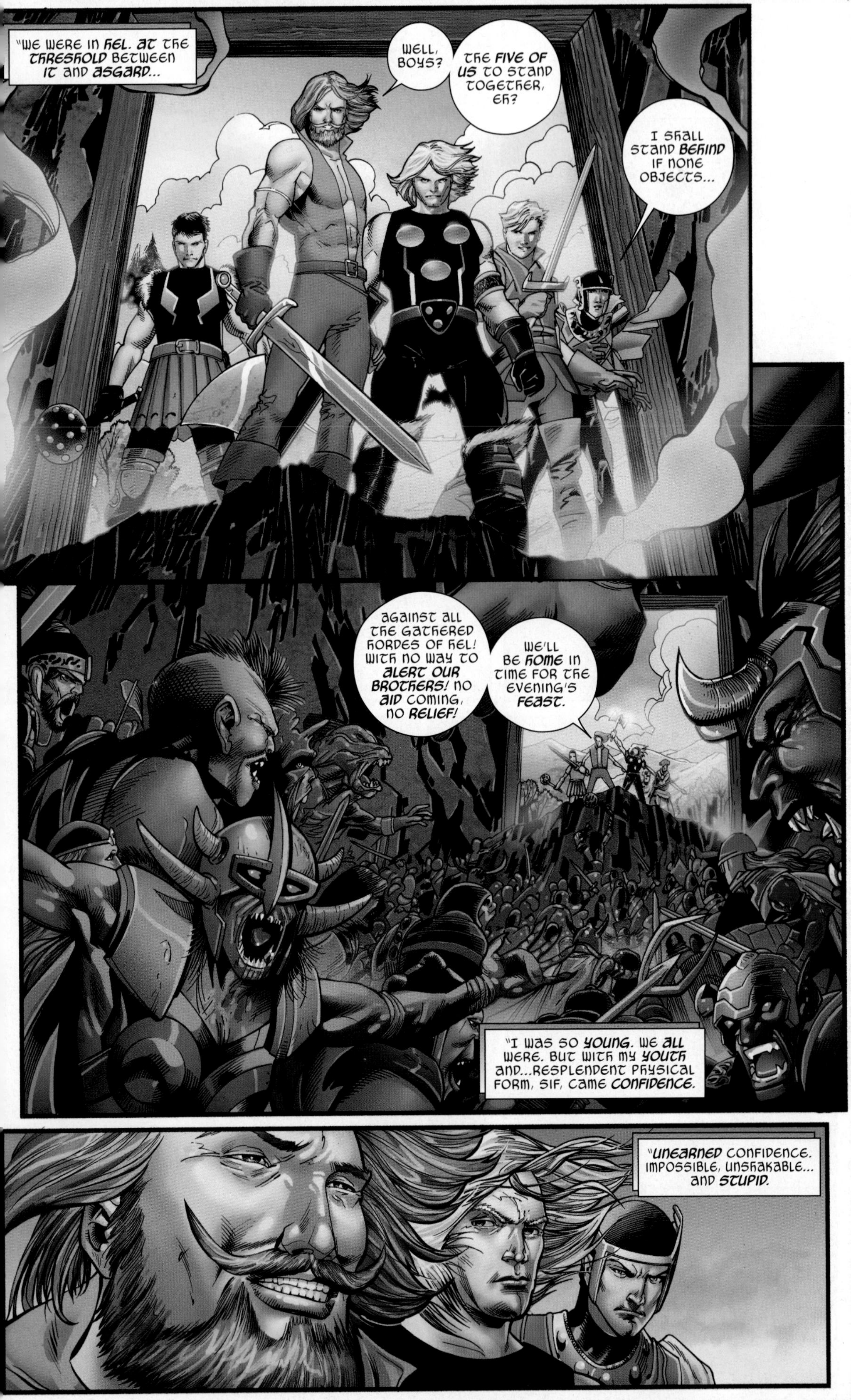

"WE WERE IN HEL. AT THE THRESHOLD BETWEEN IT AND ASGARD...
WELL, BOYS?
THE FIVE OF US TO STAND TOGETHER, EH?
I SHALL STAND BEHIND IF NONE OBJECTS...
AGAINST ALL THE GATHERED HORDES OF HEL! WITH NO WAY TO ALERT OUR BROTHERS! NO AID COMING, NO RELIEF!
WE'LL BE HOME IN TIME FOR THE EVENING'S FEAST.
"I WAS SO YOUNG. WE ALL WERE. BUT WITH MY YOUTH AND...RESPLENDENT PHYSICAL FORM, SIF, CAME CONFIDENCE.
"UNEARNED CONFIDENCE. IMPOSSIBLE, UNSHAKABLE... AND STUPID.

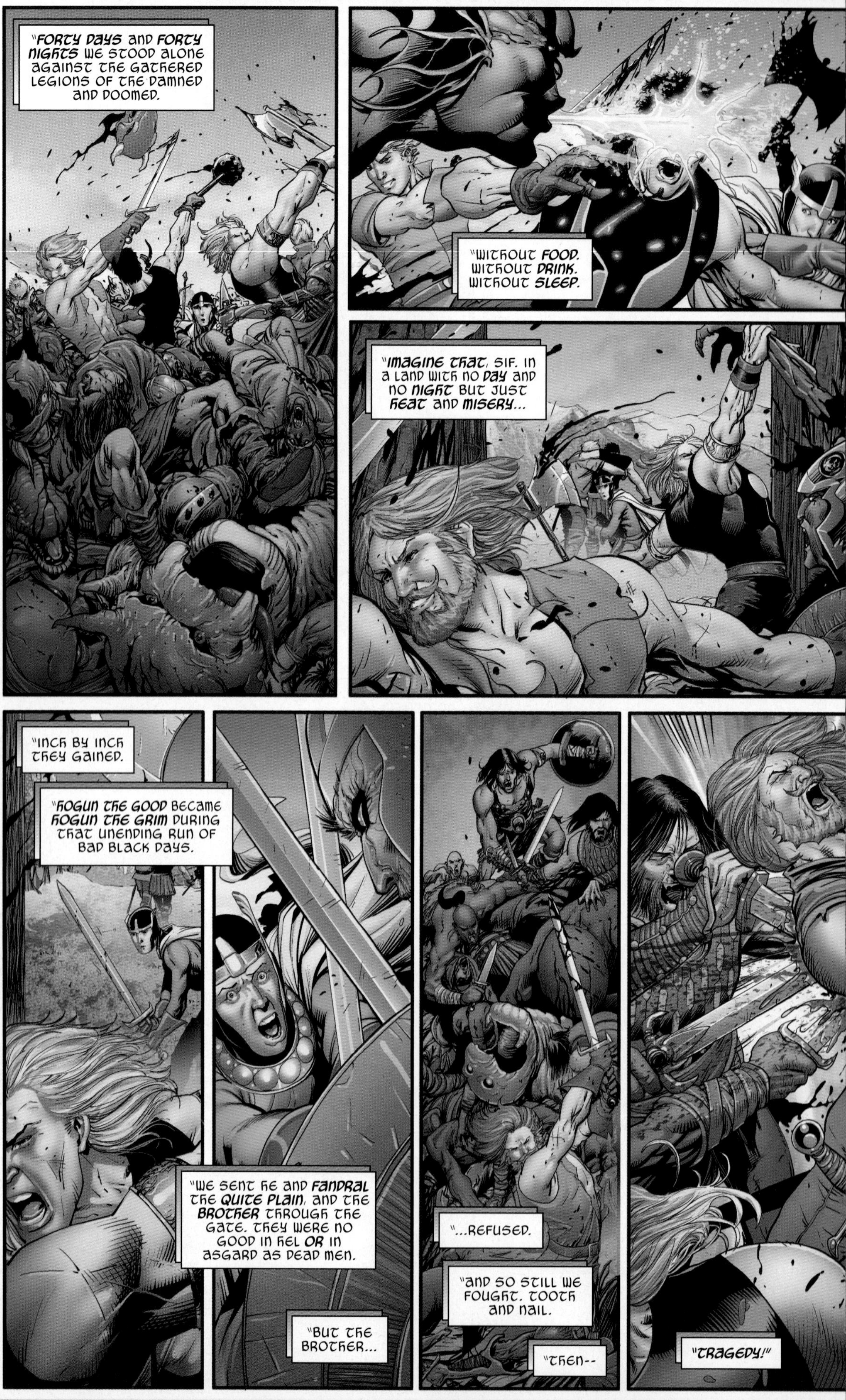
"FORTY DAYS AND FORTY NIGHTS WE STOOD ALONE AGAINST THE GATHERED LEGIONS OF THE DAMNED AND DOOMED.
"WITHOUT FOOD. WITHOUT DRINK. WITHOUT SLEEP.
"IMAGINE THAT, SIF. IN A LAND WITH NO DAY AND NO NIGHT BUT JUST HEAT AND MISERY...
"INCH BY INCH THEY GAINED.
"HOGUN THE GOOD BECAME HOGUN THE GRIM DURING THAT UNENDING RUN OF BAD BLACK DAYS.
"WE SENT HE AND FANDRAL THE QUITE PLAIN, AND THE BROTHER THROUGH THE GATE. THEY WERE NO GOOD IN HEL OR IN ASGARD AS DEAD MEN.
"BUT THE BROTHER...
"...REFUSED.
"AND SO STILL WE FOUGHT. TOOTH AND NAIL.
"THEN--
"TRAGEDY!"

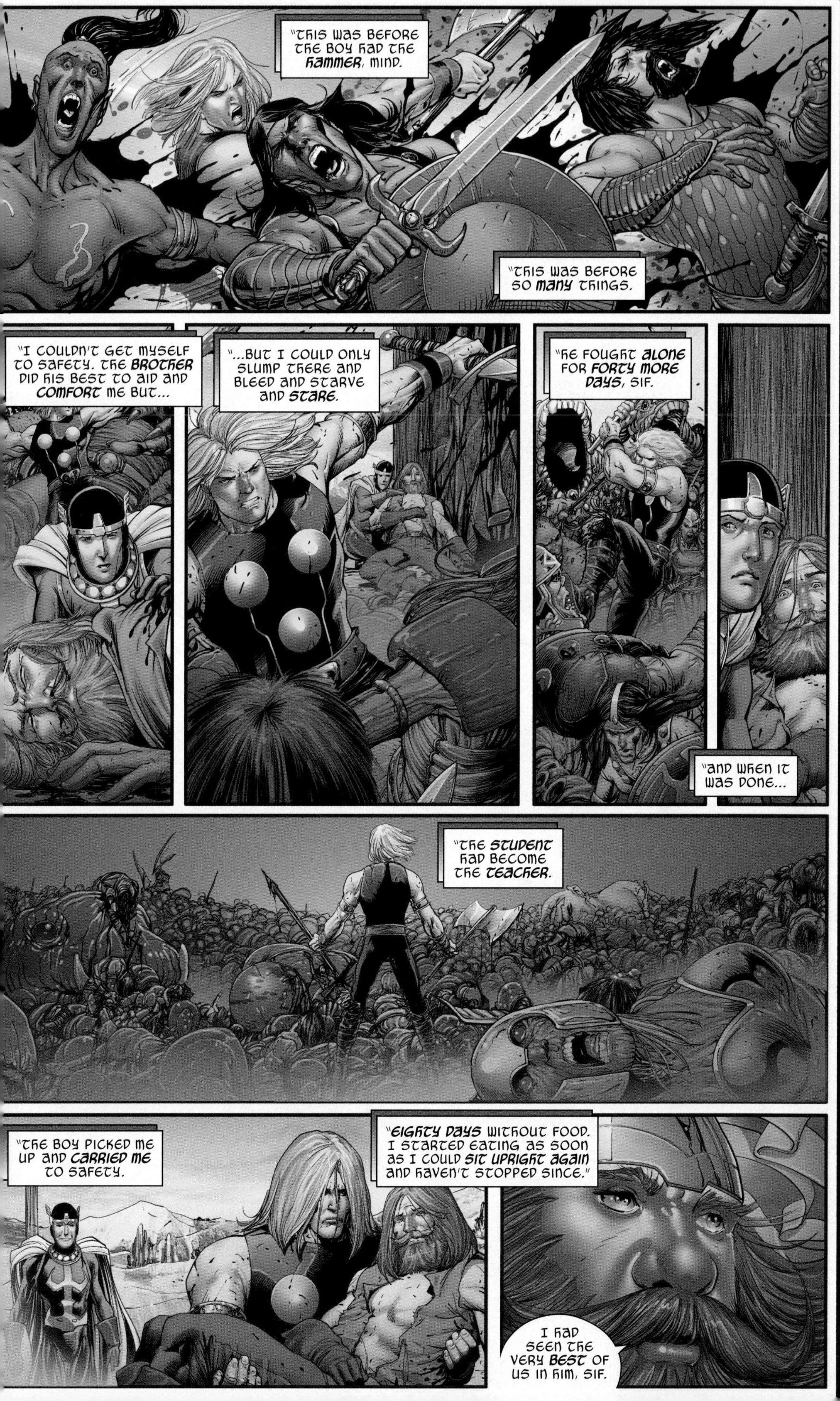
"THIS WAS BEFORE THE BOY HAD THE HAMMER, MIND.
"THIS WAS BEFORE SO MANY THINGS.
"I COULDN'T GET MYSELF TO SAFETY. THE BROTHER DID HIS BEST TO AID AND COMFORT ME BUT...
"...BUT I COULD ONLY SLUMP THERE AND BLEED AND STARVE AND STARE.
"HE FOUGHT ALONE FOR FORTY MORE DAYS, SIF.
"AND WHEN IT WAS DONE...
"THE STUDENT HAD BECOME THE TEACHER.
"THE BOY PICKED ME UP AND CARRIED ME TO SAFETY.
"EIGHTY DAYS WITHOUT FOOD. I STARTED EATING AS SOON AS I COULD SIT UPRIGHT AGAIN AND HAVEN'T STOPPED SINCE."
I HAD SEEN THE VERY BEST OF US IN HIM, SIF.

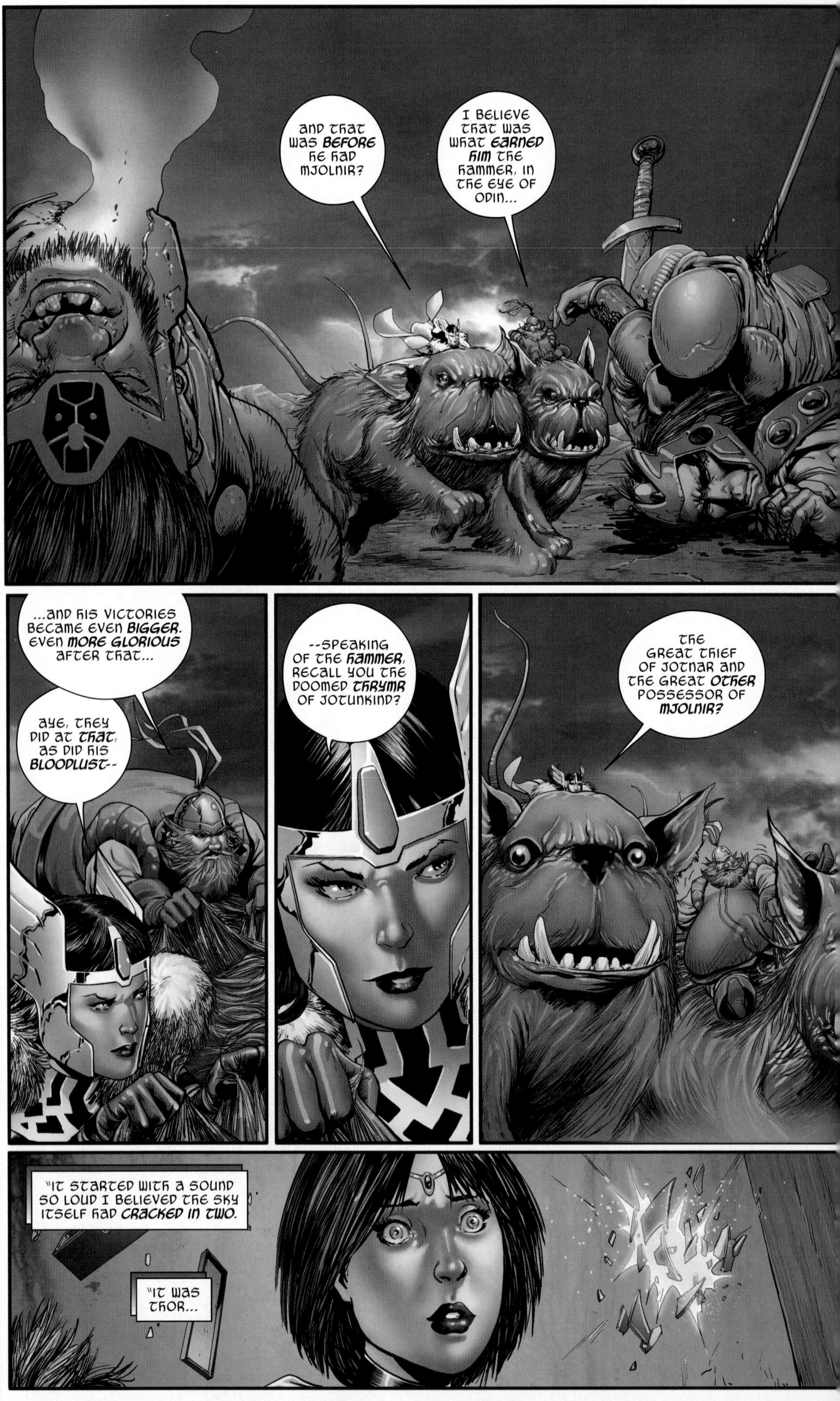

AND THAT WAS **BEFORE** HE HAD MJOLNIR?
I BELIEVE THAT WAS WHAT **EARNED HIM** THE HAMMER, IN THE EYE OF ODIN...
...AND HIS VICTORIES BECAME EVEN **BIGGER**. EVEN **MORE GLORIOUS** AFTER THAT...
AYE, THEY DID AT **THAT**, AS DID HIS **BLOODLUST**--
--SPEAKING OF THE **HAMMER**, RECALL YOU THE DOOMED **THRYMR** OF JOTUNKIND?
THE GREAT THIEF OF JOTNAR AND THE GREAT **OTHER** POSSESSOR OF **MJOLNIR?**
"IT STARTED WITH A SOUND SO LOUD I BELIEVED THE SKY ITSELF HAD **CRACKED IN TWO**.
"IT WAS THOR...

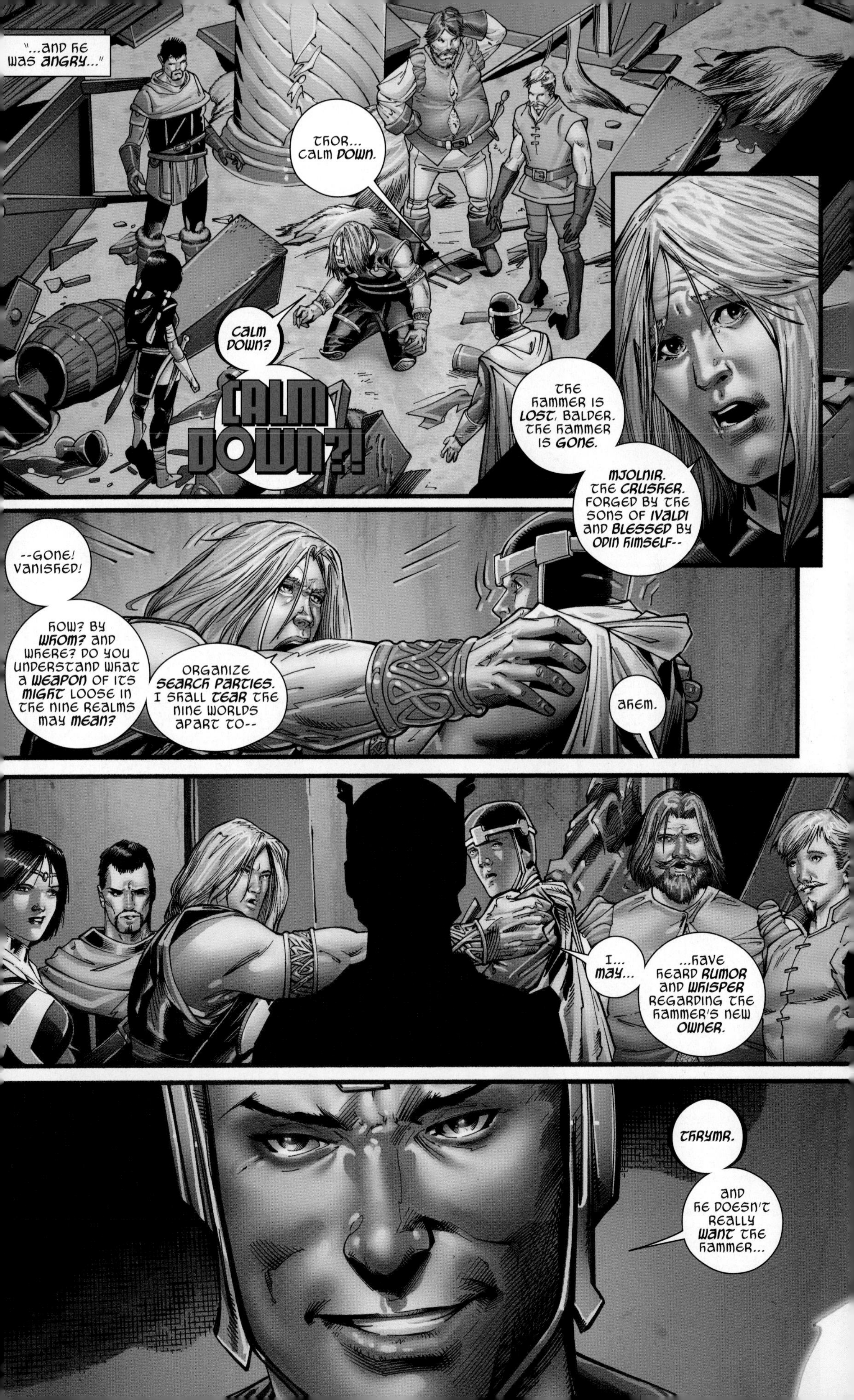
"...AND HE WAS ANGRY..."
THOR... CALM DOWN.
CALM DOWN?
CALM DOWN?!
THE HAMMER IS LOST, BALDER. THE HAMMER IS GONE.
MJOLNIR. THE CRUSHER. FORGED BY THE SONS OF IVALDI AND BLESSED BY ODIN HIMSELF--
--GONE! VANISHED!
HOW? BY WHOM? AND WHERE? DO YOU UNDERSTAND WHAT A WEAPON OF ITS MIGHT LOOSE IN THE NINE REALMS MAY MEAN?
ORGANIZE SEARCH PARTIES. I SHALL TEAR THE NINE WORLDS APART TO--
AHEM.
I... MAY...
...HAVE HEARD RUMOR AND WHISPER REGARDING THE HAMMER'S NEW OWNER.
THRYMR.
AND HE DOESN'T REALLY WANT THE HAMMER...

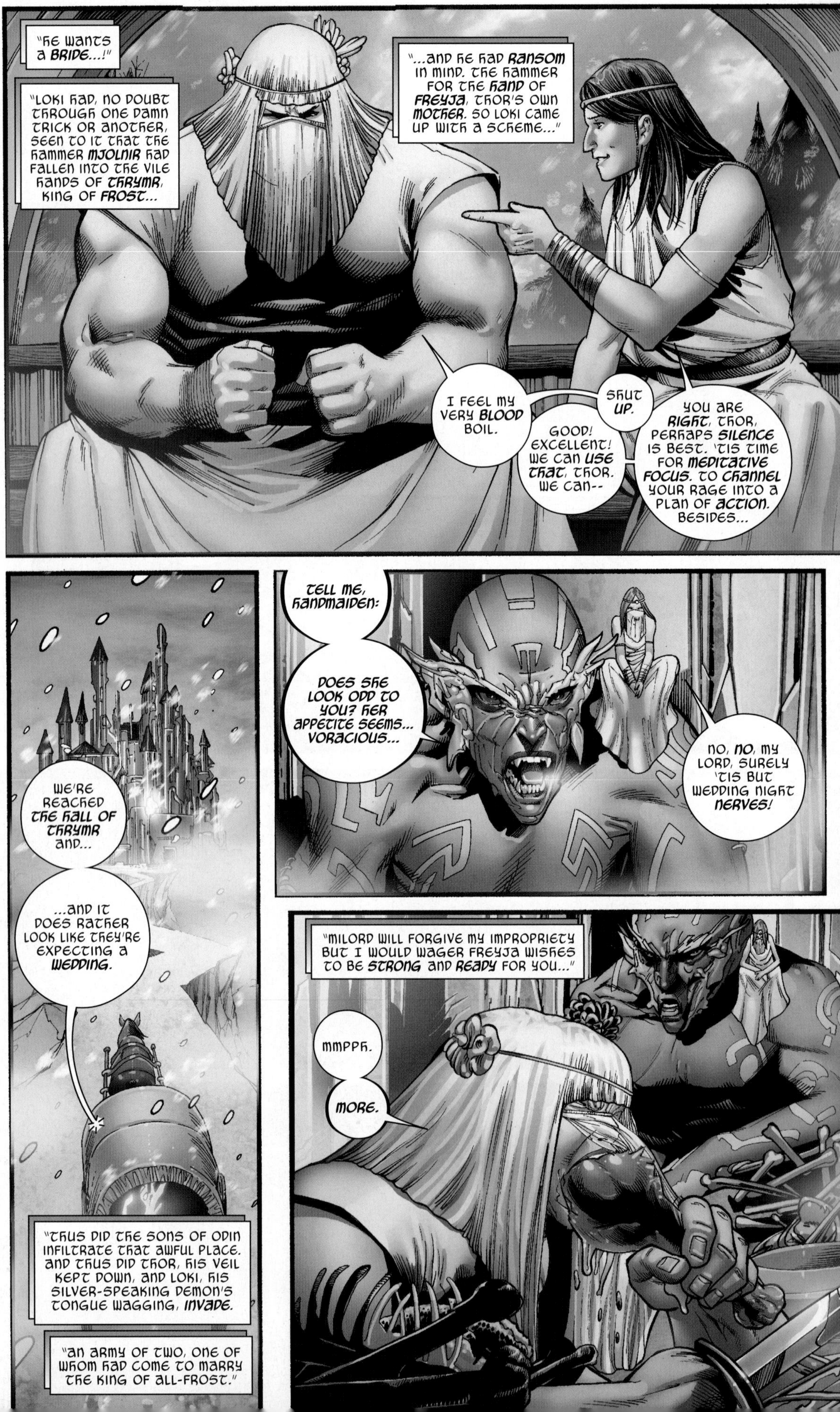
"HE WANTS A BRIDE...!"
"LOKI HAD, NO DOUBT THROUGH ONE DAMN TRICK OR ANOTHER, SEEN TO IT THAT THE HAMMER MJOLNIR HAD FALLEN INTO THE VILE HANDS OF THRYMR, KING OF FROST...
"...AND HE HAD RANSOM IN MIND. THE HAMMER FOR THE HAND OF FREYJA, THOR'S OWN MOTHER. SO LOKI CAME UP WITH A SCHEME..."
I FEEL MY VERY BLOOD BOIL.
GOOD! EXCELLENT! WE CAN USE THAT, THOR. WE CAN--
SHUT UP.
YOU ARE RIGHT, THOR, PERHAPS SILENCE IS BEST. 'TIS TIME FOR MEDITATIVE FOCUS. TO CHANNEL YOUR RAGE INTO A PLAN OF ACTION. BESIDES...
WE'RE REACHED THE HALL OF THRYMR AND...
...AND IT DOES RATHER LOOK LIKE THEY'RE EXPECTING A WEDDING.
"THUS DID THE SONS OF ODIN INFILTRATE THAT AWFUL PLACE. AND THUS DID THOR, HIS VEIL KEPT DOWN, AND LOKI, HIS SILVER-SPEAKING DEMON'S TONGUE WAGGING, INVADE.
"AN ARMY OF TWO, ONE OF WHOM HAD COME TO MARRY THE KING OF ALL-FROST."
TELL ME, HANDMAIDEN:
DOES SHE LOOK ODD TO YOU? HER APPETITE SEEMS... VORACIOUS...
NO, NO, MY LORD, SURELY 'TIS BUT WEDDING NIGHT NERVES!
"MILORD WILL FORGIVE MY IMPROPRIETY BUT I WOULD WAGER FREYJA WISHES TO BE STRONG AND READY FOR YOU..."
MMPPH.
MORE.

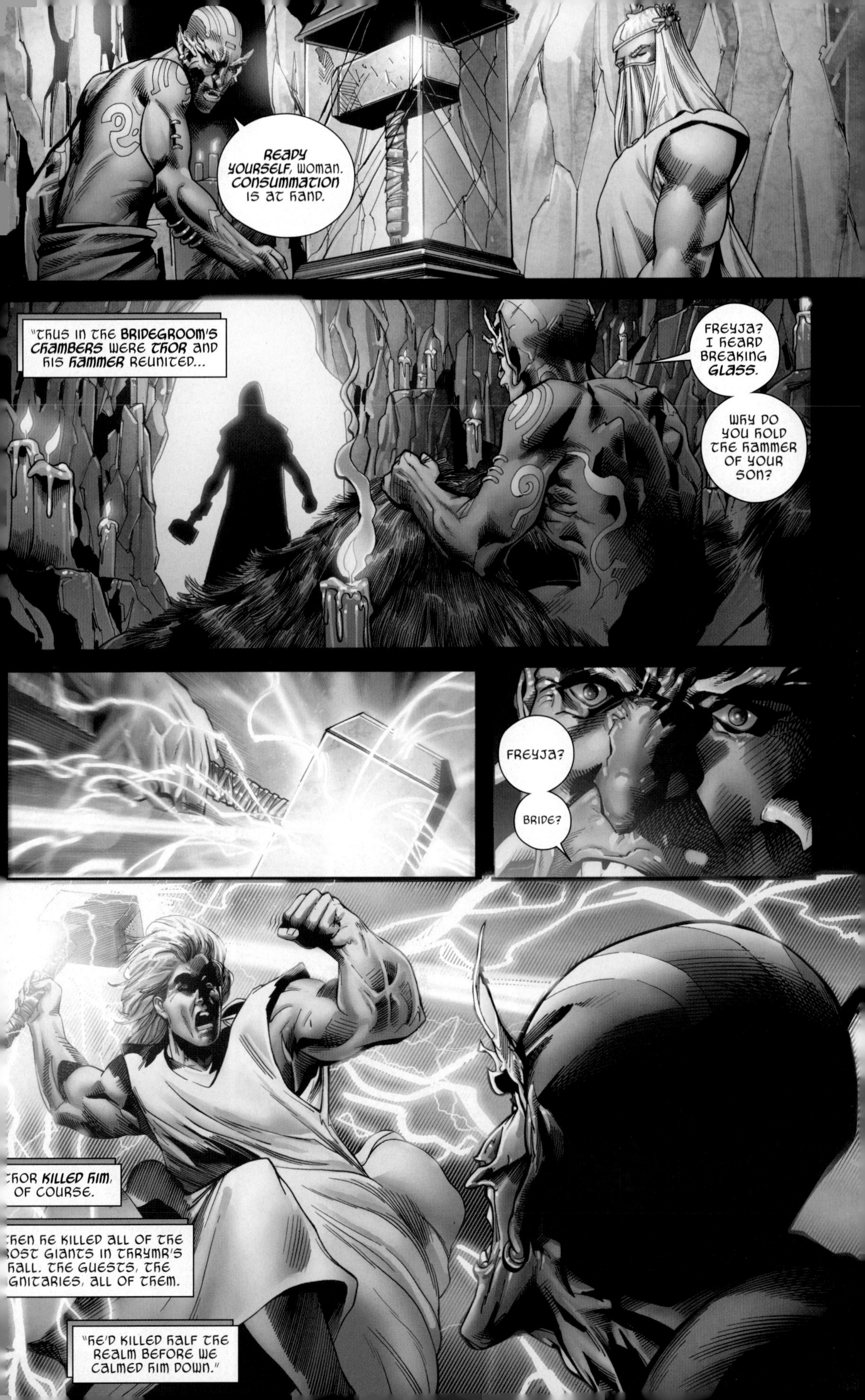
READY YOURSELF, WOMAN. CONSUMMATION IS AT HAND.
"THUS IN THE BRIDEGROOM'S CHAMBERS WERE THOR AND HIS HAMMER REUNITED...
FREYJA? I HEARD BREAKING GLASS.
WHY DO YOU HOLD THE HAMMER OF YOUR SON?
FREYJA?
BRIDE?
THOR KILLED HIM, OF COURSE.
THEN HE KILLED ALL OF THE FROST GIANTS IN THRYMR'S HALL. THE GUESTS, THE DIGNITARIES, ALL OF THEM.
"HE'D KILLED HALF THE REALM BEFORE WE CALMED HIM DOWN."

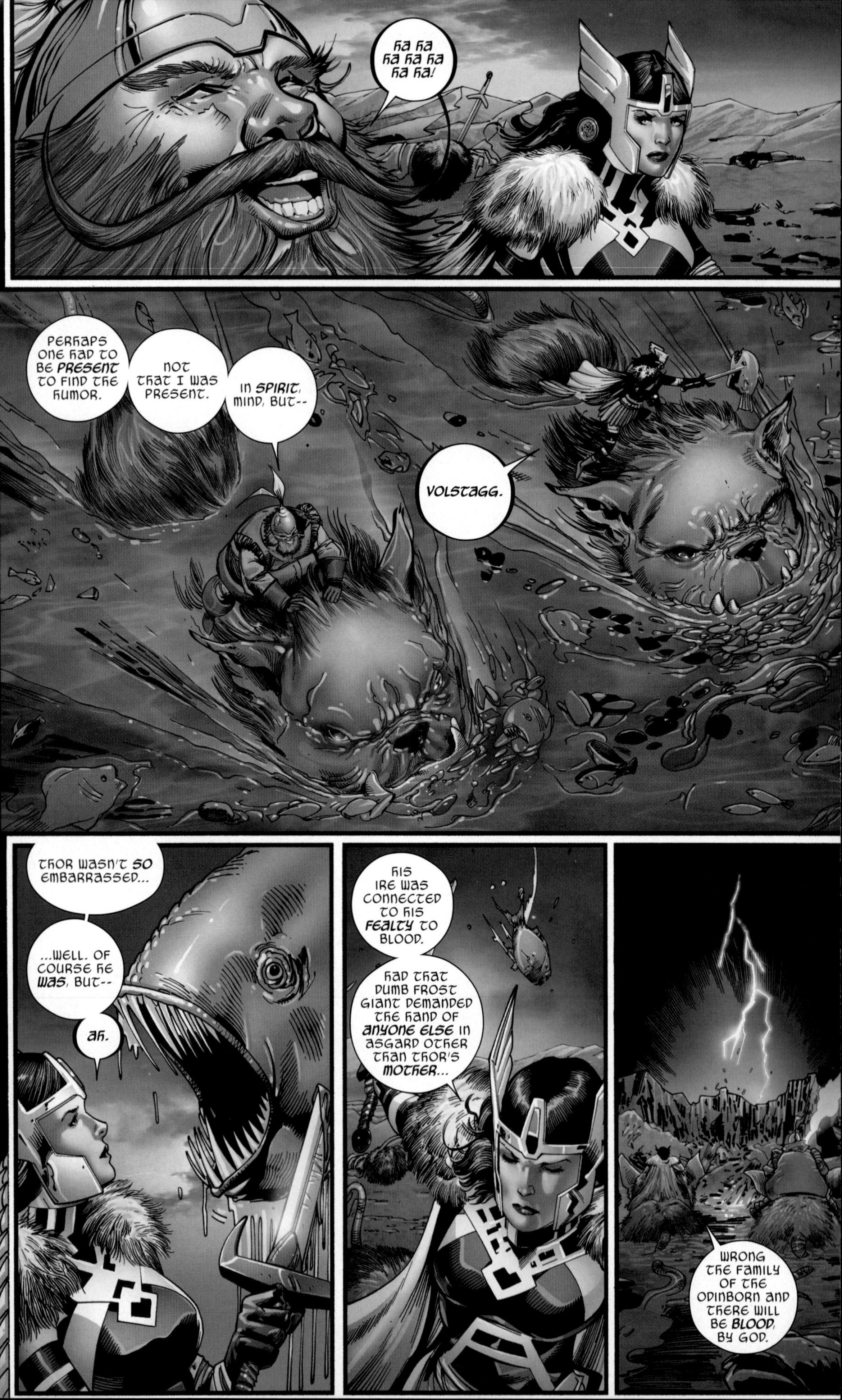

HA HA HA HA HA HA HA!
PERHAPS ONE HAD TO BE PRESENT TO FIND THE HUMOR.
NOT THAT I WAS PRESENT.
IN SPIRIT, MIND, BUT--
VOLSTAGG.
THOR WASN'T SO EMBARRASSED...
...WELL. OF COURSE HE WAS, BUT--
AH.
HIS IRE WAS CONNECTED TO HIS FEALTY TO BLOOD.
HAD THAT DUMB FROST GIANT DEMANDED THE HAND OF ANYONE ELSE IN ASGARD OTHER THAN THOR'S MOTHER...
WRONG THE FAMILY OF THE ODINBORN AND THERE WILL BE BLOOD, BY GOD.

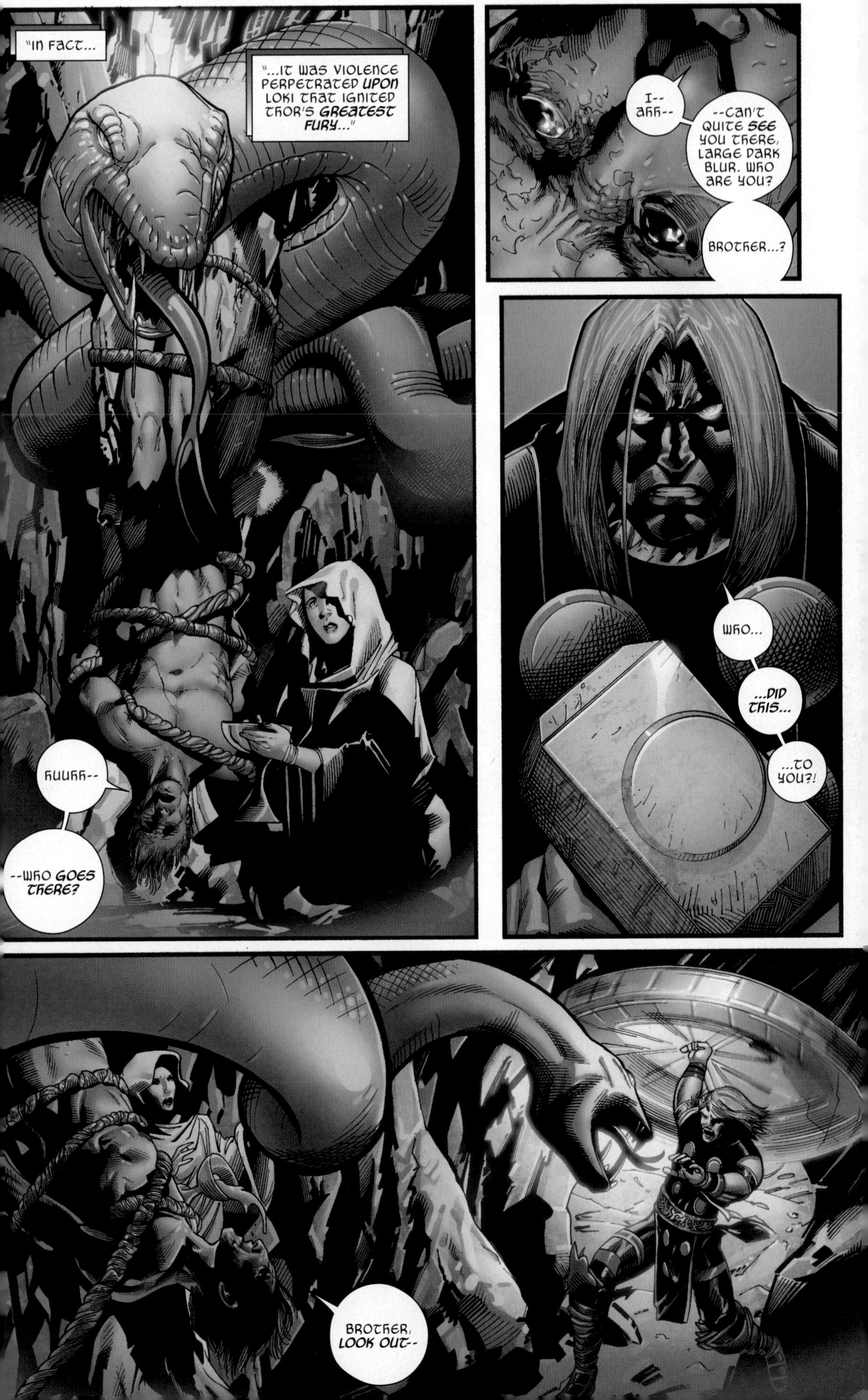
"IN FACT...
"...IT WAS VIOLENCE PERPETRATED UPON LOKI THAT IGNITED THOR'S GREATEST FURY..."
HUUHH--
--WHO GOES THERE?
I-- AHH--
--CAN'T QUITE SEE YOU THERE, LARGE DARK BLUR. WHO ARE YOU?
BROTHER...?
WHO...
...DID THIS...
...TO YOU?!
BROTHER, LOOK OUT--

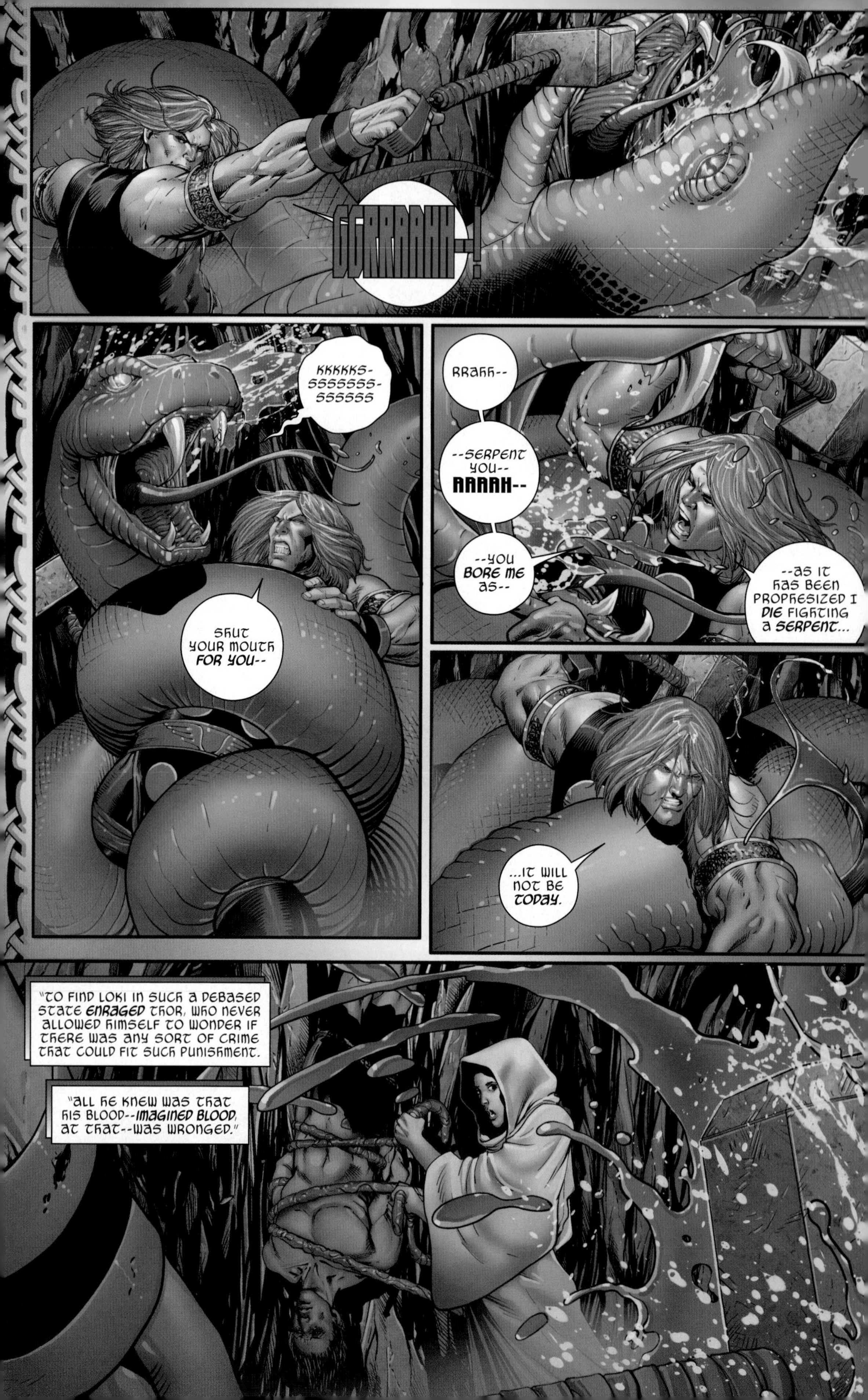
GGRRAAHH--!
KKKKKS-SSSSSSS-SSSSSS
SHUT YOUR MOUTH FOR YOU--
RRAHH--
--SERPENT YOU--
AAARAH--
--YOU BORE ME AS--
--AS IT HAS BEEN PROPHESIZED I DIE FIGHTING A SERPENT...
...IT WILL NOT BE TODAY.
"TO FIND LOKI IN SUCH A DEBASED STATE ENRAGED THOR, WHO NEVER ALLOWED HIMSELF TO WONDER IF THERE WAS ANY SORT OF CRIME THAT COULD FIT SUCH PUNISHMENT.
"ALL HE KNEW WAS THAT HIS BLOOD--IMAGINED BLOOD, AT THAT--WAS WRONGED."

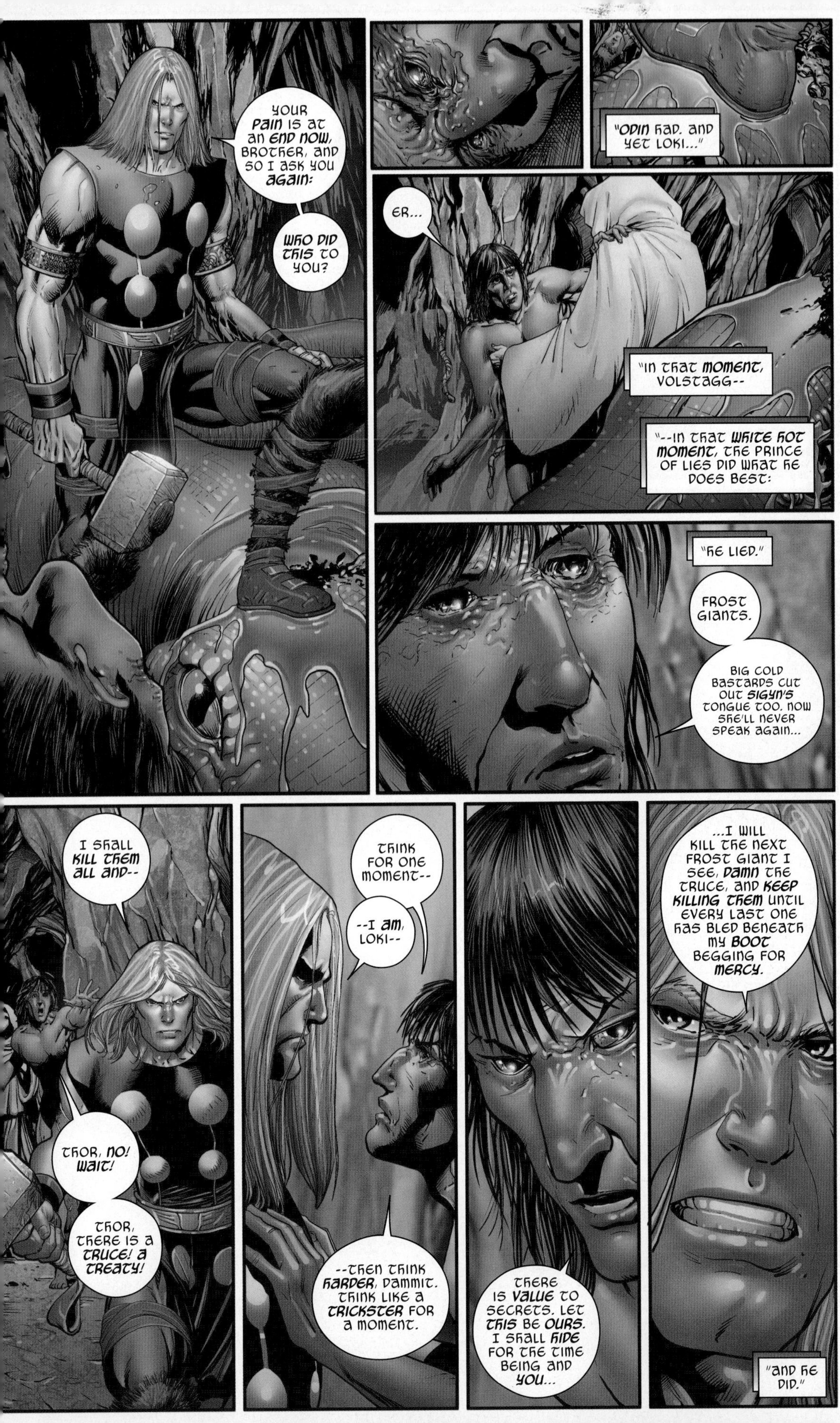
YOUR PAIN IS AT AN END NOW, BROTHER, AND SO I ASK YOU AGAIN:
WHO DID THIS TO YOU?
"ODIN HAD. AND YET LOKI..."
ER...
"IN THAT MOMENT, VOLSTAGG--
"--IN THAT WHITE HOT MOMENT, THE PRINCE OF LIES DID WHAT HE DOES BEST:
"HE LIED."
FROST GIANTS.
BIG COLD BASTARDS CUT OUT SIGYN'S TONGUE TOO. NOW SHE'LL NEVER SPEAK AGAIN...
I SHALL KILL THEM ALL AND--
THOR, NO! WAIT!
THOR, THERE IS A TRUCE! A TREATY!
THINK FOR ONE MOMENT--
--I AM, LOKI--
--THEN THINK HARDER, DAMMIT. THINK LIKE A TRICKSTER FOR A MOMENT.
THERE IS VALUE TO SECRETS. LET THIS BE OURS. I SHALL HIDE FOR THE TIME BEING AND YOU...
...I WILL KILL THE NEXT FROST GIANT I SEE, DAMN THE TRUCE, AND KEEP KILLING THEM UNTIL EVERY LAST ONE HAS BLED BENEATH MY BOOT BEGGING FOR MERCY.
"AND HE DID."

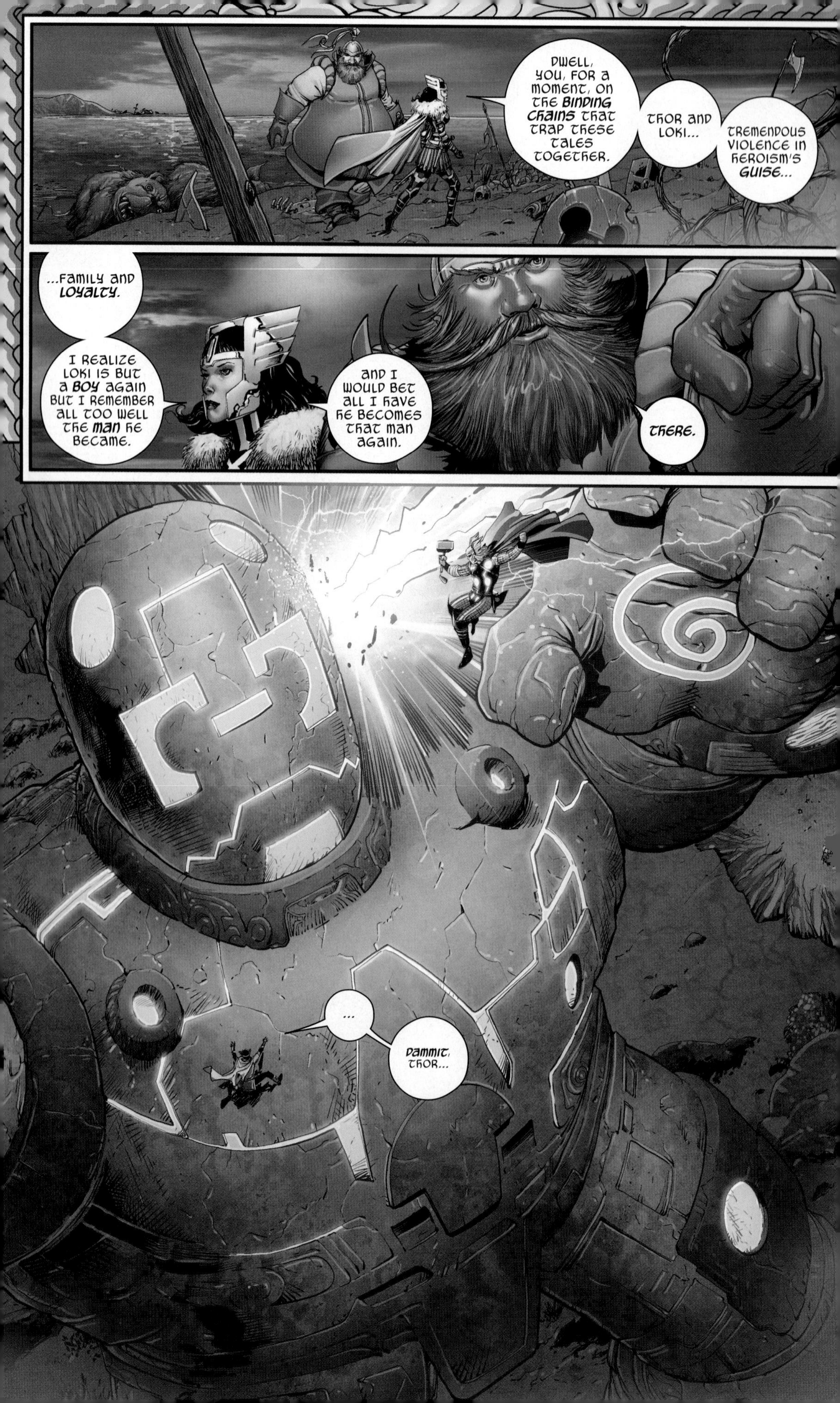
DWELL, YOU, FOR A MOMENT, ON THE BINDING CHAINS THAT TRAP THESE TALES TOGETHER.
THOR AND LOKI...
TREMENDOUS VIOLENCE IN HEROISM'S GUISE...
...FAMILY AND LOYALTY.
I REALIZE LOKI IS BUT A BOY AGAIN BUT I REMEMBER ALL TOO WELL THE MAN HE BECAME.
AND I WOULD BET ALL I HAVE HE BECOMES THAT MAN AGAIN.
THERE.
...
DAMMIT, THOR...

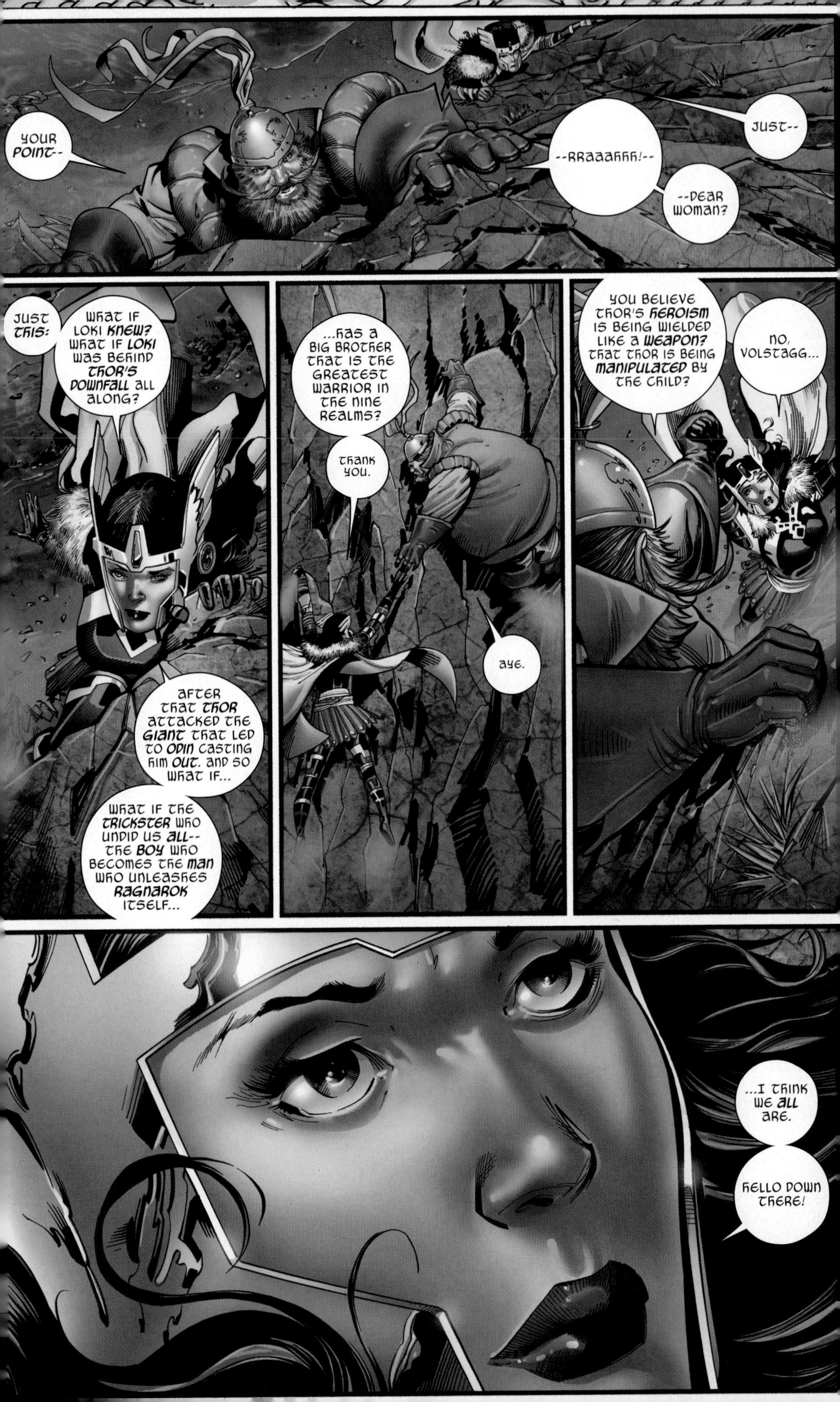

YOUR POINT--
JUST--
--RRAAAHHH!--
--DEAR WOMAN?
JUST THIS:
WHAT IF LOKI KNEW? WHAT IF LOKI WAS BEHIND THOR'S DOWNFALL ALL ALONG?
AFTER THAT THOR ATTACKED THE GIANT THAT LED TO ODIN CASTING HIM OUT. AND SO WHAT IF...
WHAT IF THE TRICKSTER WHO UNDID US ALL--THE BOY WHO BECOMES THE MAN WHO UNLEASHES RAGNAROK ITSELF...
...HAS A BIG BROTHER THAT IS THE GREATEST WARRIOR IN THE NINE REALMS?
THANK YOU.
AYE.
YOU BELIEVE THOR'S HEROISM IS BEING WIELDED LIKE A WEAPON? THAT THOR IS BEING MANIPULATED BY THE CHILD?
NO, VOLSTAGG...
...I THINK WE ALL ARE.
HELLO DOWN THERE!

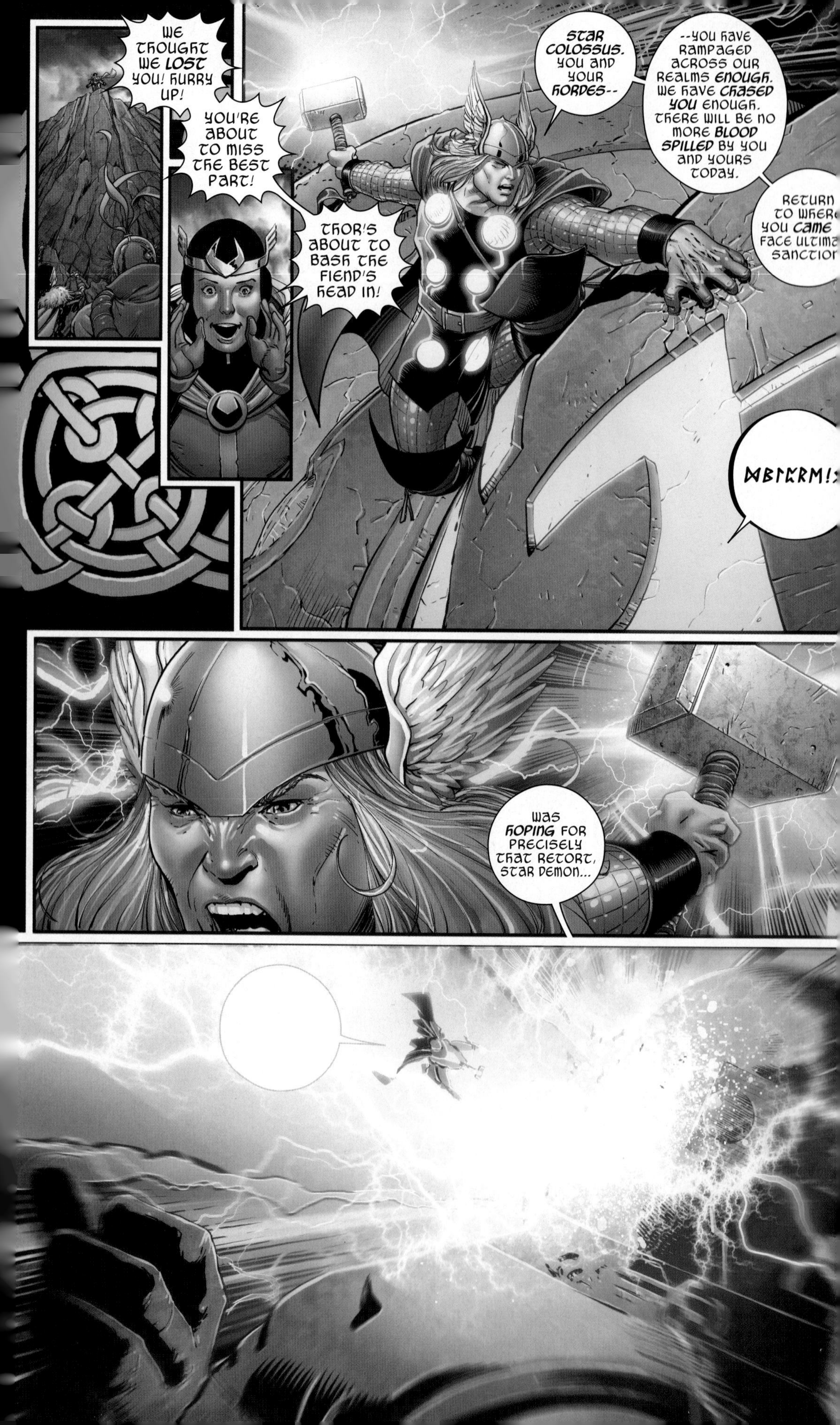
WE THOUGHT WE LOST YOU! HURRY UP!
YOU'RE ABOUT TO MISS THE BEST PART!
THOR'S ABOUT TO BASH THE FIEND'S HEAD IN!
STAR COLOSSUS. YOU AND YOUR HORDES--
--YOU HAVE RAMPAGED ACROSS OUR REALMS ENOUGH. WE HAVE CHASED YOU ENOUGH. THERE WILL BE NO MORE BLOOD SPILLED BY YOU AND YOURS TODAY.
RETURN TO WHER YOU CAME FACE ULTIMA SANCTIO
WAS HOPING FOR PRECISELY THAT RETORT, STAR DEMON...

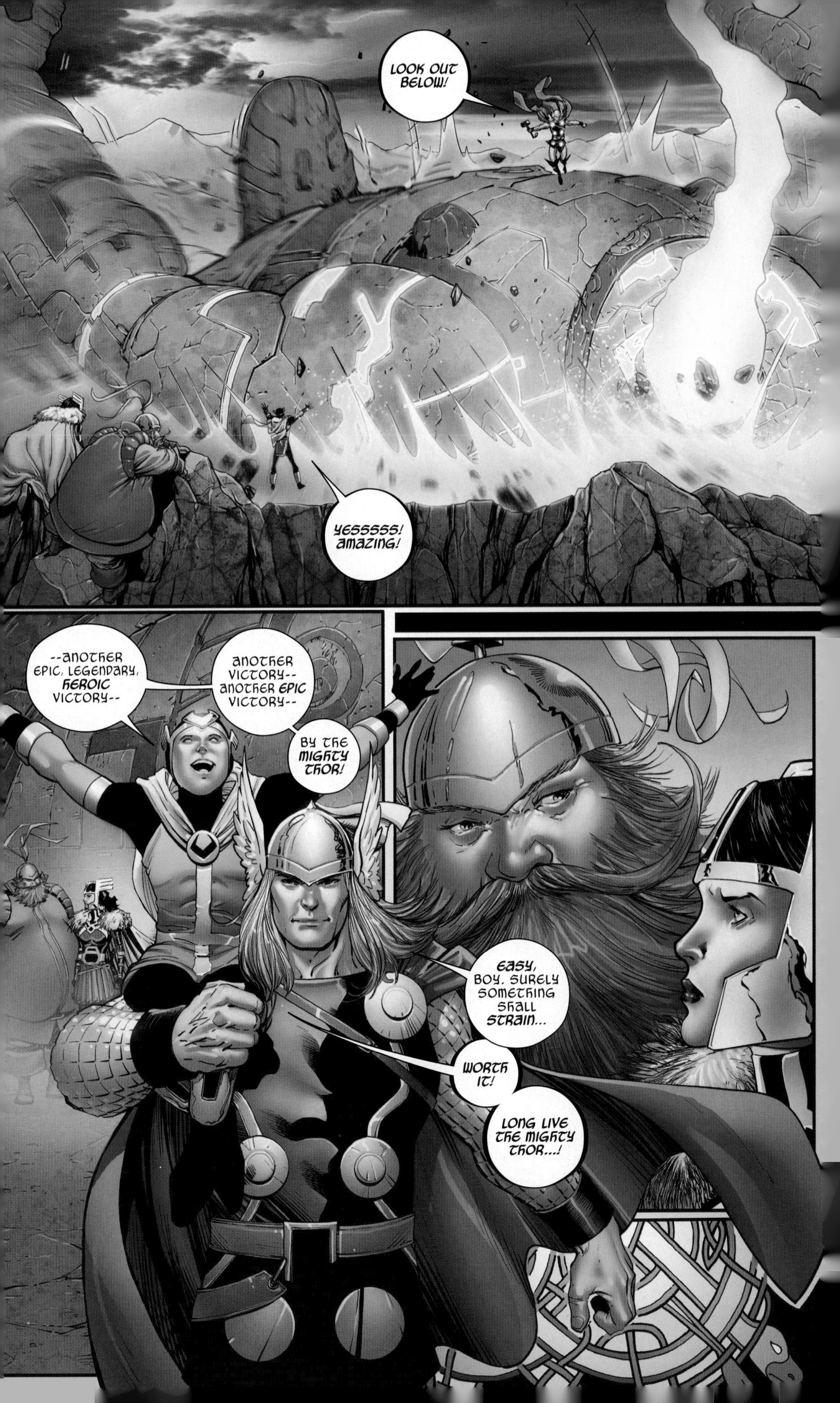
LOOK OUT BELOW!
YESSSSS! AMAZING!
--ANOTHER EPIC, LEGENDARY, HEROIC VICTORY--
ANOTHER VICTORY-- ANOTHER EPIC VICTORY--
BY THE MIGHTY THOR!
EASY, BOY. SURELY SOMETHING SHALL STRAIN...
WORTH IT!
LONG LIVE THE MIGHTY THOR...!

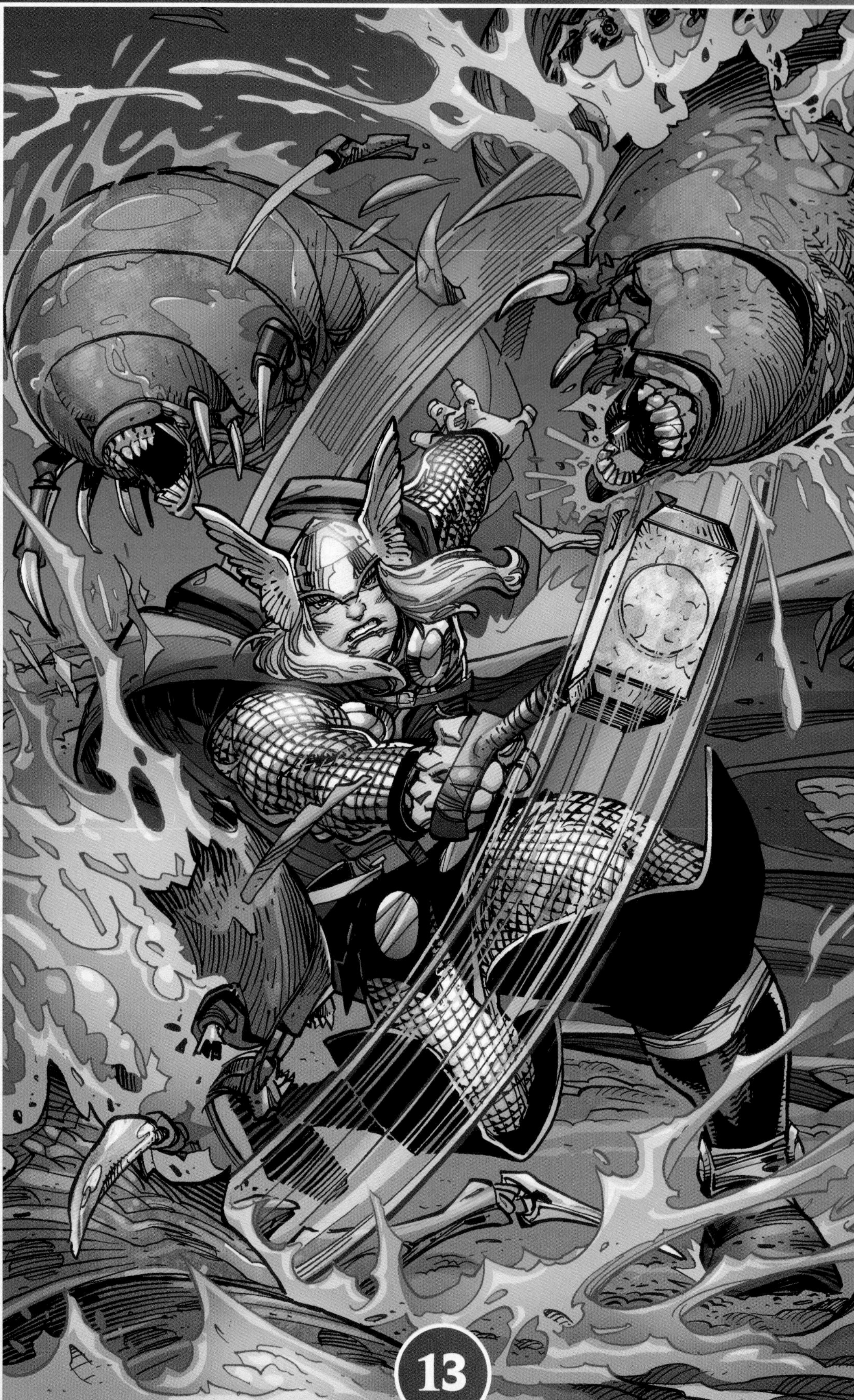

He is the son of Asgard, a golden city floating high above the Earth's surface, the capital of a new republic of Nine Worlds led by the All-Mother. He is the God of Thunder. He is an Avenger. He is—

The Mighty Thor

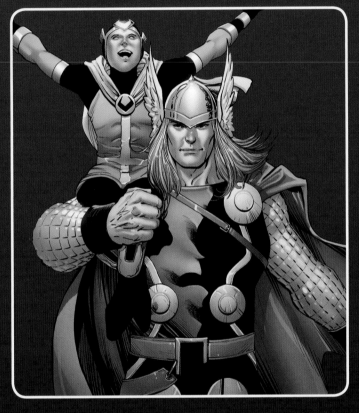

Thor died to save the world from Fear Itself, and Asgard lay broken. By breaking a sinister enchantment, Thor returned to save the fledgling republic of Asgardia from itself, and peace was restored. The would-be usurpers of the ruling All-Mother have been undone. The city of Asgard has returned to the skies, its full splendor renewed. The Nine Realms are calm, but for the God of Thunder, that calm can only mean that somewhere, a storm is brewing.

Years ago, as a lesson to a young and headstrong Thor, the All-Father joined the Thunder God to the mortal form of Doctor Donald Blake to teach Thor humility and compassion.

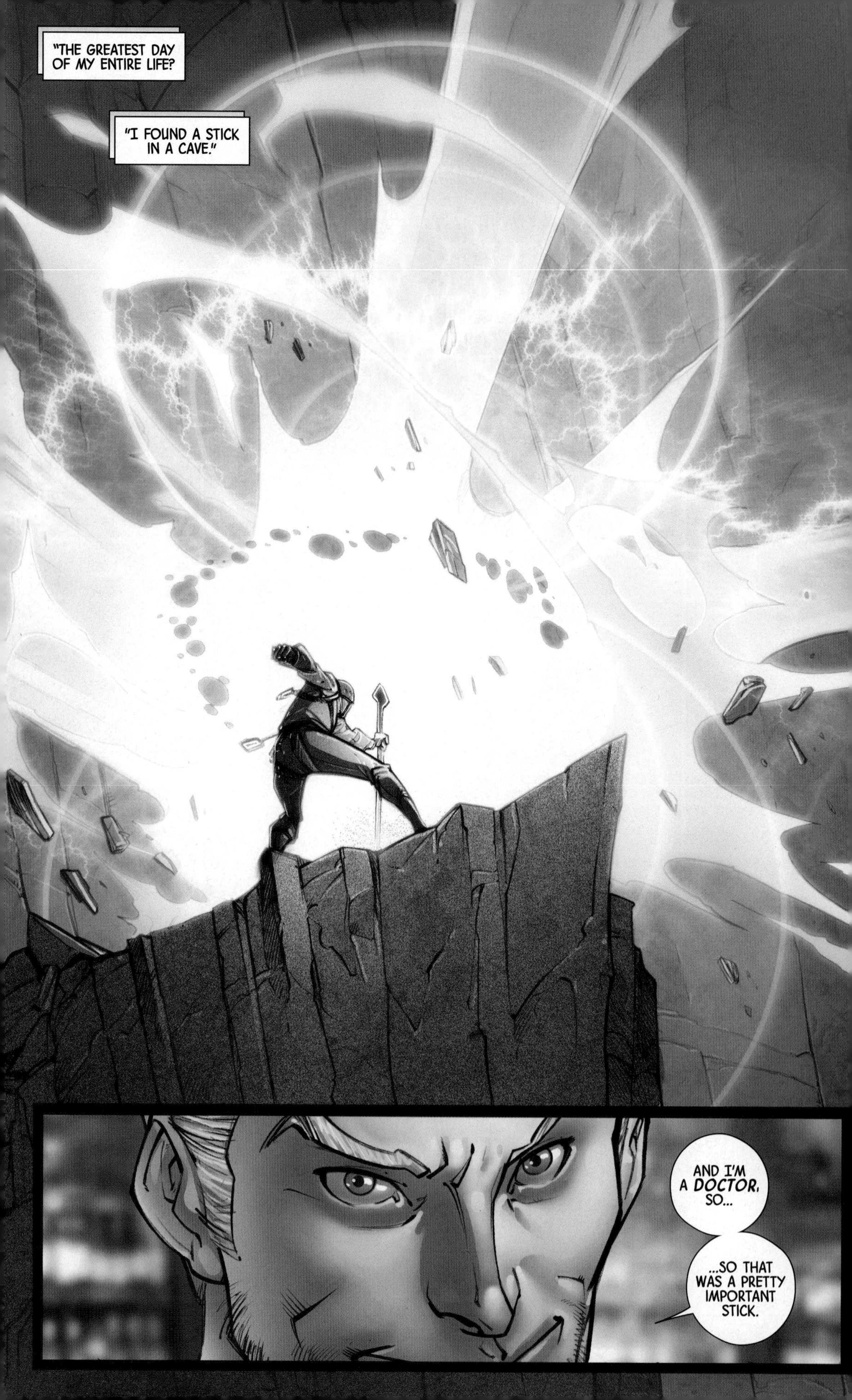
"THE GREATEST DAY OF MY ENTIRE LIFE?
"I FOUND A STICK IN A CAVE."
AND I'M A *DOCTOR*, SO...
...SO THAT WAS A PRETTY IMPORTANT STICK.

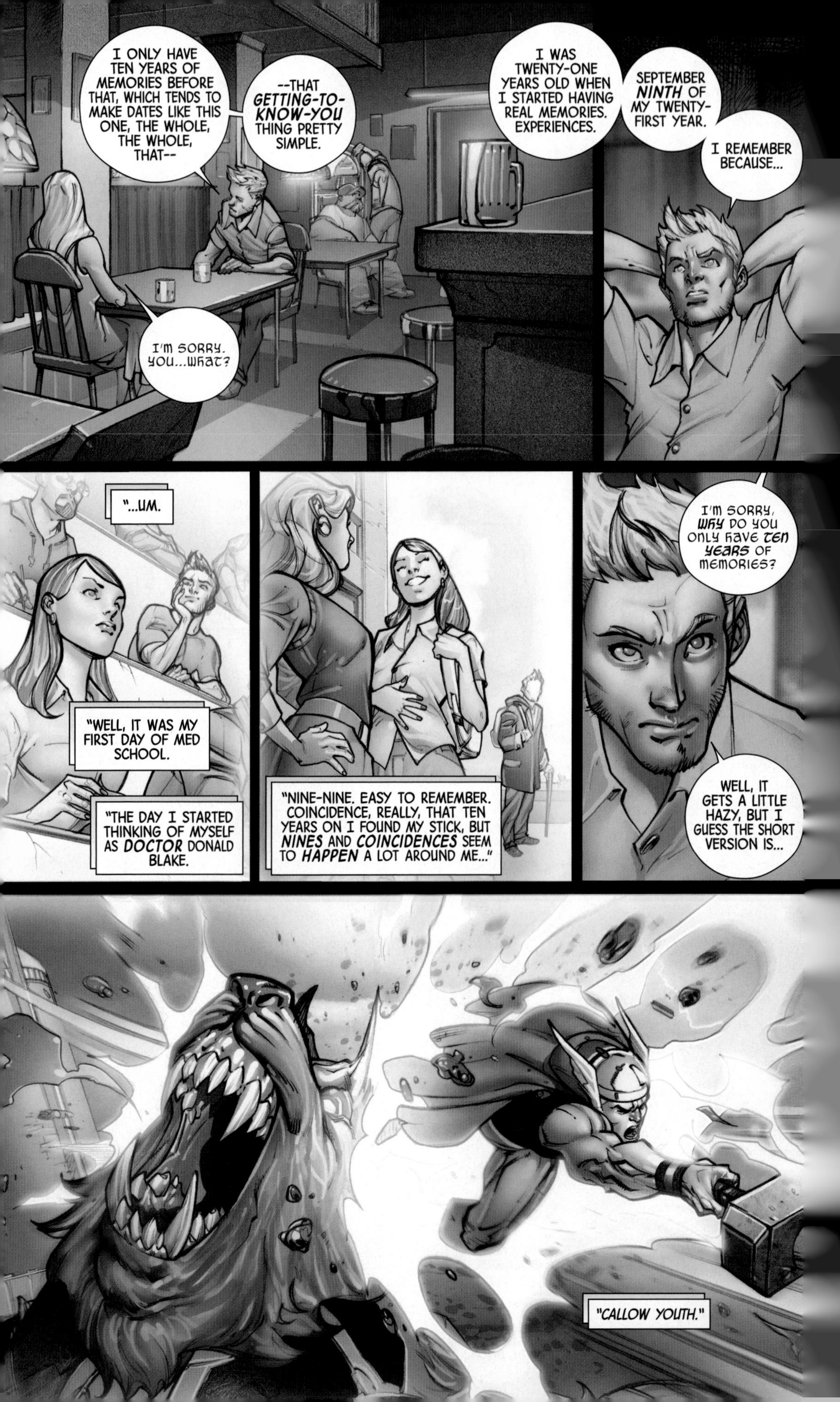

I ONLY HAVE TEN YEARS OF MEMORIES BEFORE THAT, WHICH TENDS TO MAKE DATES LIKE THIS ONE, THE WHOLE, THE WHOLE, THAT--
--THAT GETTING-TO-KNOW-YOU THING PRETTY SIMPLE.
I'M SORRY. YOU...WHAT?
I WAS TWENTY-ONE YEARS OLD WHEN I STARTED HAVING REAL MEMORIES. EXPERIENCES.
SEPTEMBER NINTH OF MY TWENTY-FIRST YEAR.
I REMEMBER BECAUSE...
"...UM.
"WELL, IT WAS MY FIRST DAY OF MED SCHOOL.
"THE DAY I STARTED THINKING OF MYSELF AS DOCTOR DONALD BLAKE.
"NINE-NINE. EASY TO REMEMBER. COINCIDENCE, REALLY, THAT TEN YEARS ON I FOUND MY STICK, BUT NINES AND COINCIDENCES SEEM TO HAPPEN A LOT AROUND ME..."
I'M SORRY, WHY DO YOU ONLY HAVE TEN YEARS OF MEMORIES?
WELL, IT GETS A LITTLE HAZY, BUT I GUESS THE SHORT VERSION IS...
"CALLOW YOUTH."

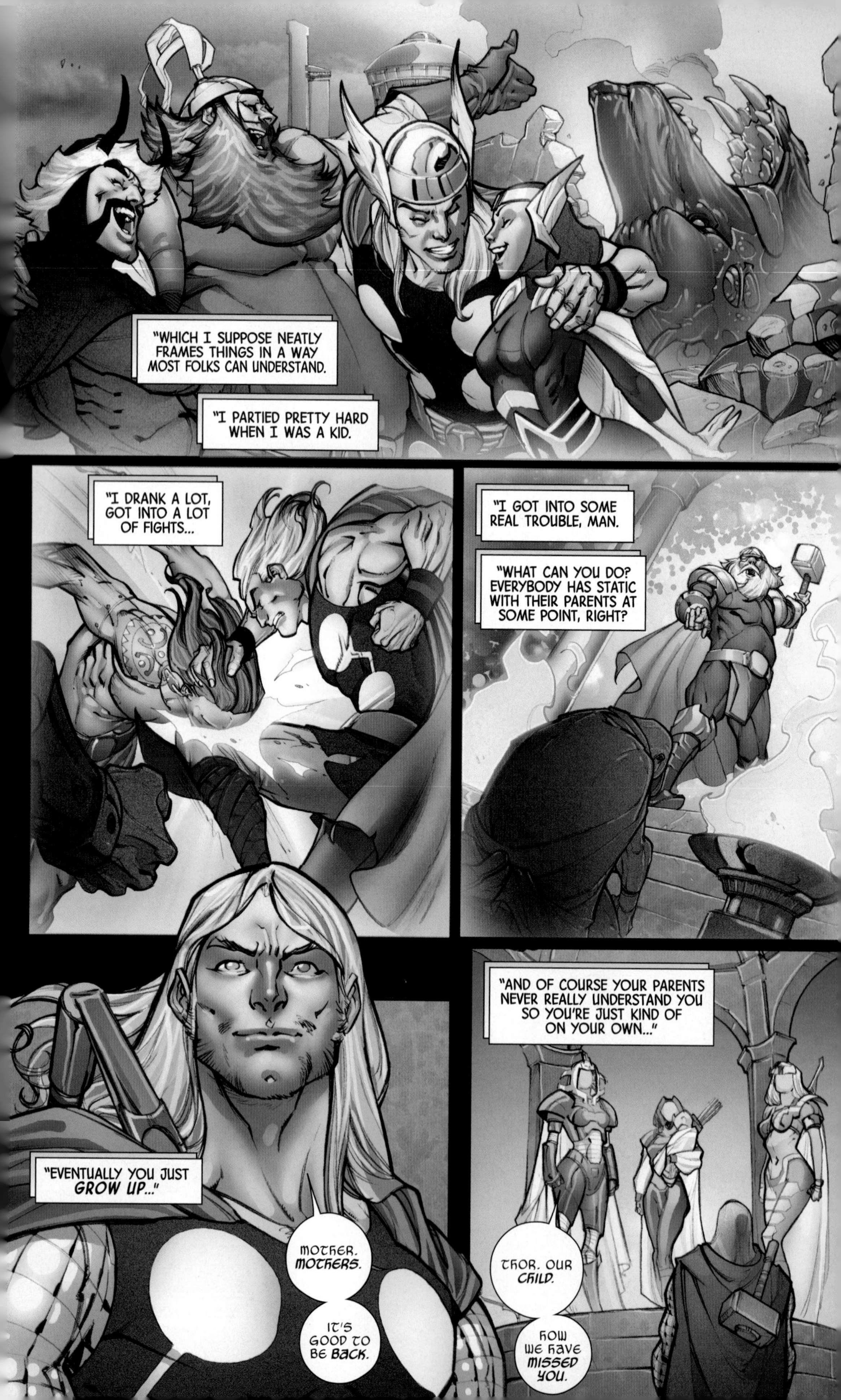
"WHICH I SUPPOSE NEATLY FRAMES THINGS IN A WAY MOST FOLKS CAN UNDERSTAND.
"I PARTIED PRETTY HARD WHEN I WAS A KID.
"I DRANK A LOT, GOT INTO A LOT OF FIGHTS...
"I GOT INTO SOME REAL TROUBLE, MAN.
"WHAT CAN YOU DO? EVERYBODY HAS STATIC WITH THEIR PARENTS AT SOME POINT, RIGHT?
"EVENTUALLY YOU JUST *GROW UP*..."
MOTHER. *MOTHERS.*
IT'S GOOD TO BE *BACK*.
"AND OF COURSE YOUR PARENTS NEVER REALLY UNDERSTAND YOU SO YOU'RE JUST KIND OF ON YOUR OWN..."
THOR. OUR *CHILD*.
HOW WE HAVE *MISSED* YOU.

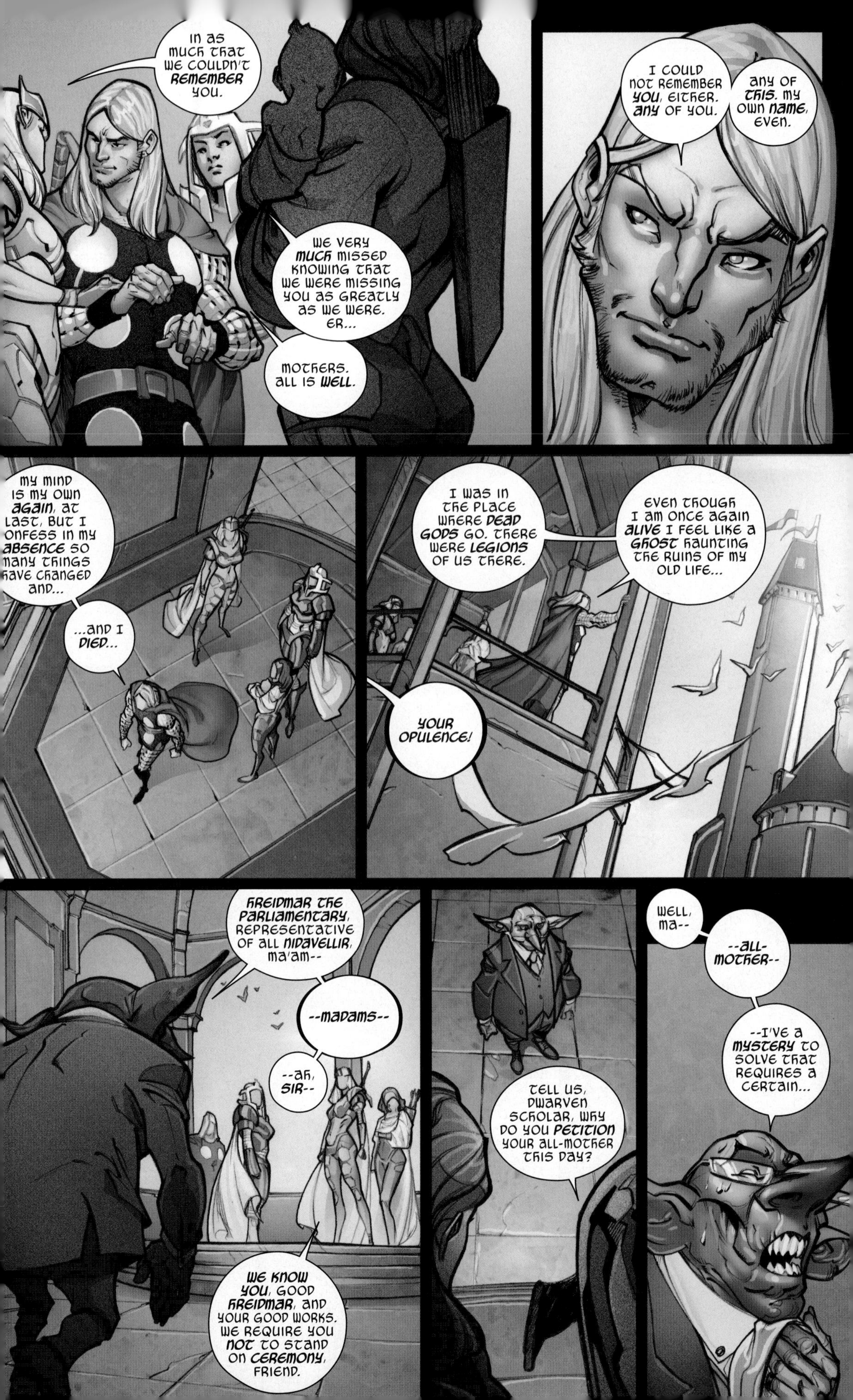
In as much that we couldn't remember you.
We very much missed knowing that we were missing you as greatly as we were. Er...
Mothers. All is well.
I could not remember you, either. Any of you.
Any of this. My own name, even.
My mind is my own again, at last, but I onfess in my absence so many things have changed and...
...and I died...
I was in the place where dead gods go. There were legions of us there.
Even though I am once again alive I feel like a ghost haunting the ruins of my old life...
Your opulence!
Hreidmar the Parliamentary, representative of all Nidavellir, ma'am--
--madams--
--ah, sir--
We know you, good Hreidmar, and your good works. We require you not to stand on ceremony, friend.
Tell us, dwarven scholar, why do you petition your All-Mother this day?
Well, ma--
--All-Mother--
--I've a mystery to solve that requires a certain...

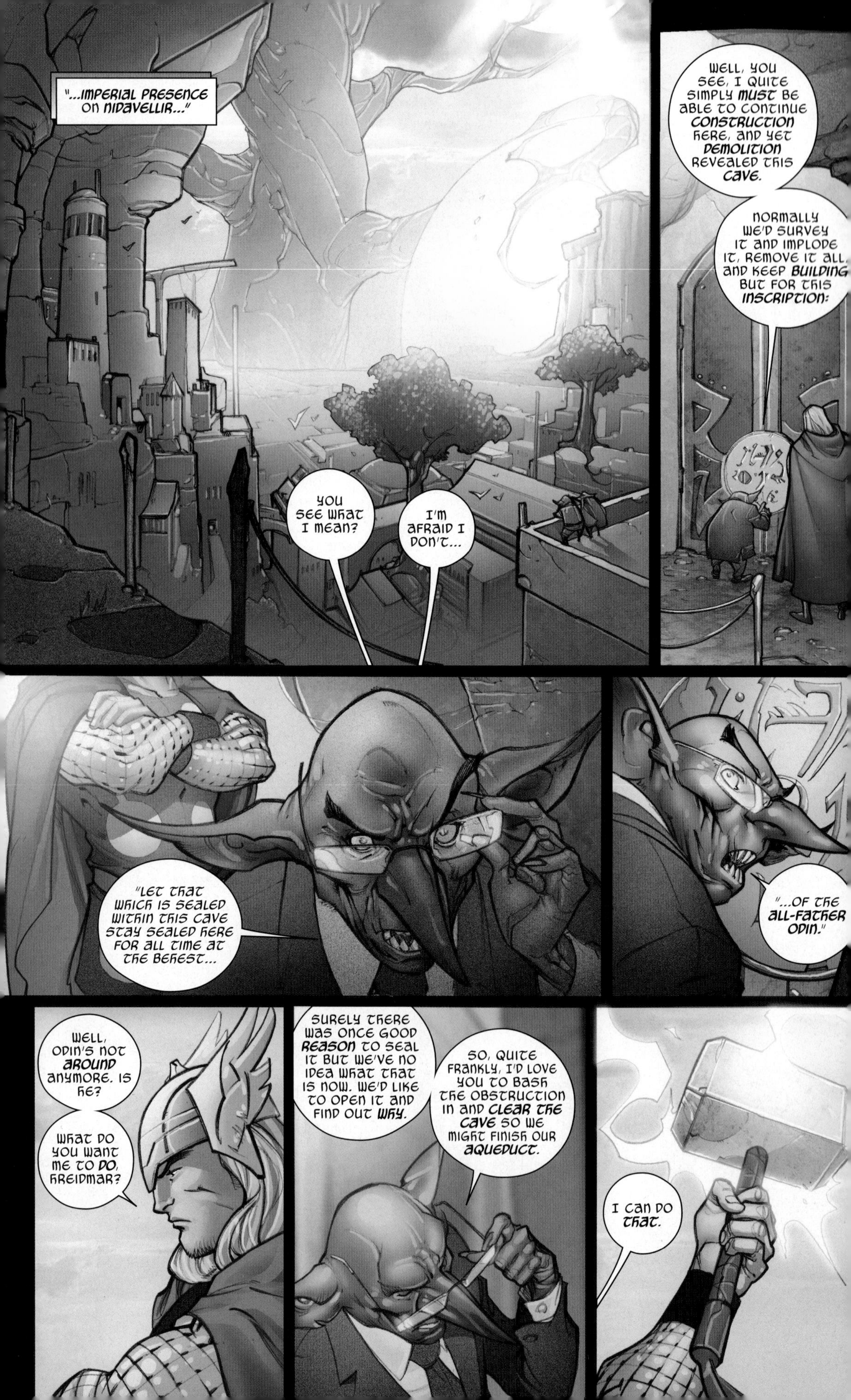
"...IMPERIAL PRESENCE ON NIDAVELLIR..."
YOU SEE WHAT I MEAN?
I'M AFRAID I DON'T...
WELL, YOU SEE, I QUITE SIMPLY MUST BE ABLE TO CONTINUE CONSTRUCTION HERE, AND YET DEMOLITION REVEALED THIS CAVE.
NORMALLY WE'D SURVEY IT AND IMPLODE IT, REMOVE IT ALL, AND KEEP BUILDING BUT FOR THIS INSCRIPTION:
"LET THAT WHICH IS SEALED WITHIN THIS CAVE STAY SEALED HERE FOR ALL TIME AT THE BEHEST...
"...OF THE ALL-FATHER ODIN."
WELL, ODIN'S NOT AROUND ANYMORE. IS HE?
WHAT DO YOU WANT ME TO DO, HREIDMAR?
SURELY THERE WAS ONCE GOOD REASON TO SEAL IT BUT WE'VE NO IDEA WHAT THAT IS NOW. WE'D LIKE TO OPEN IT AND FIND OUT WHY.
SO, QUITE FRANKLY, I'D LOVE YOU TO BASH THE OBSTRUCTION IN AND CLEAR THE CAVE SO WE MIGHT FINISH OUR AQUEDUCT.
I CAN DO THAT.

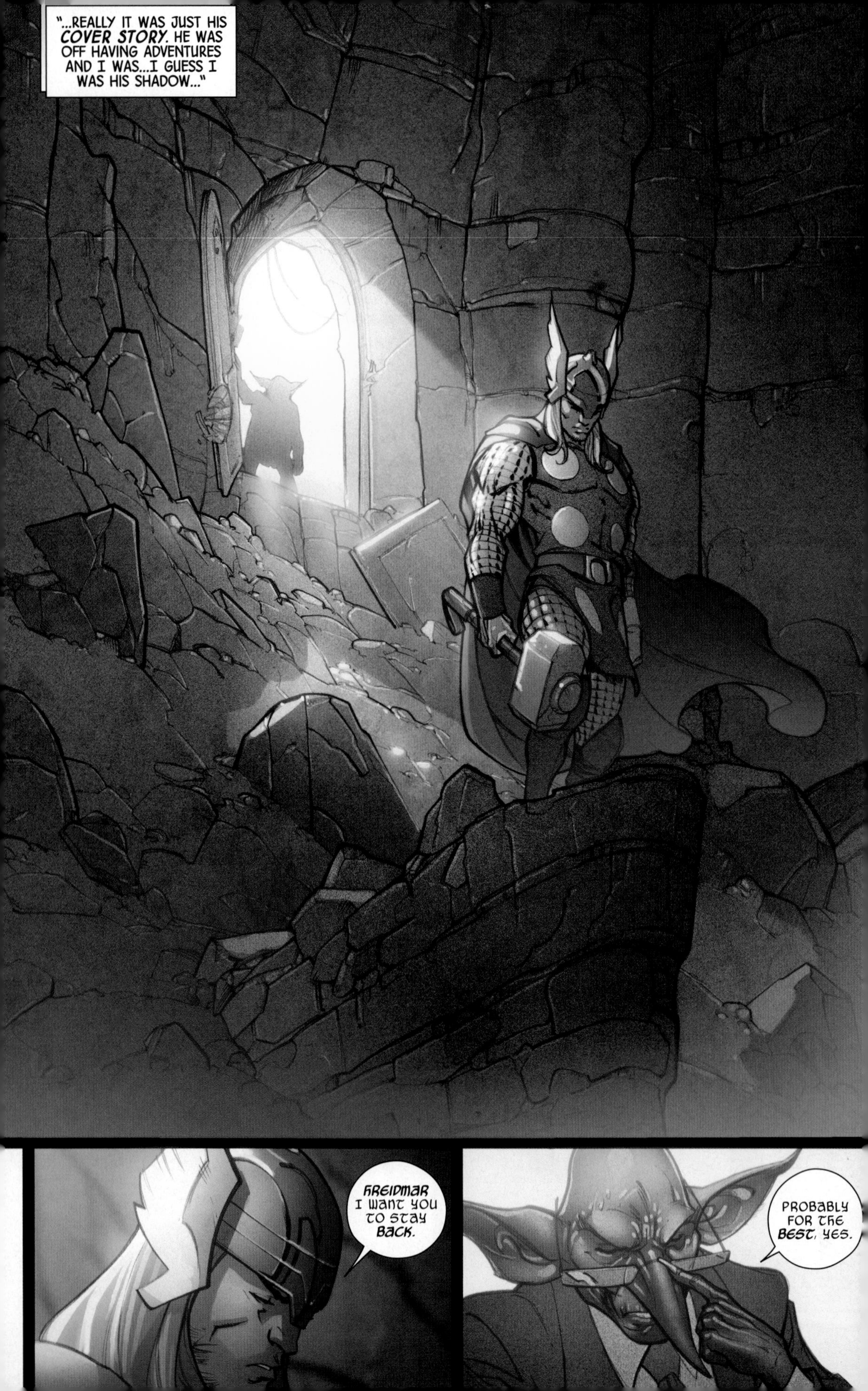
"...REALLY IT WAS JUST HIS COVER STORY. HE WAS OFF HAVING ADVENTURES AND I WAS...I GUESS I WAS HIS SHADOW..."
FREIDMAR I WANT YOU TO STAY BACK.
PROBABLY FOR THE BEST, YES.

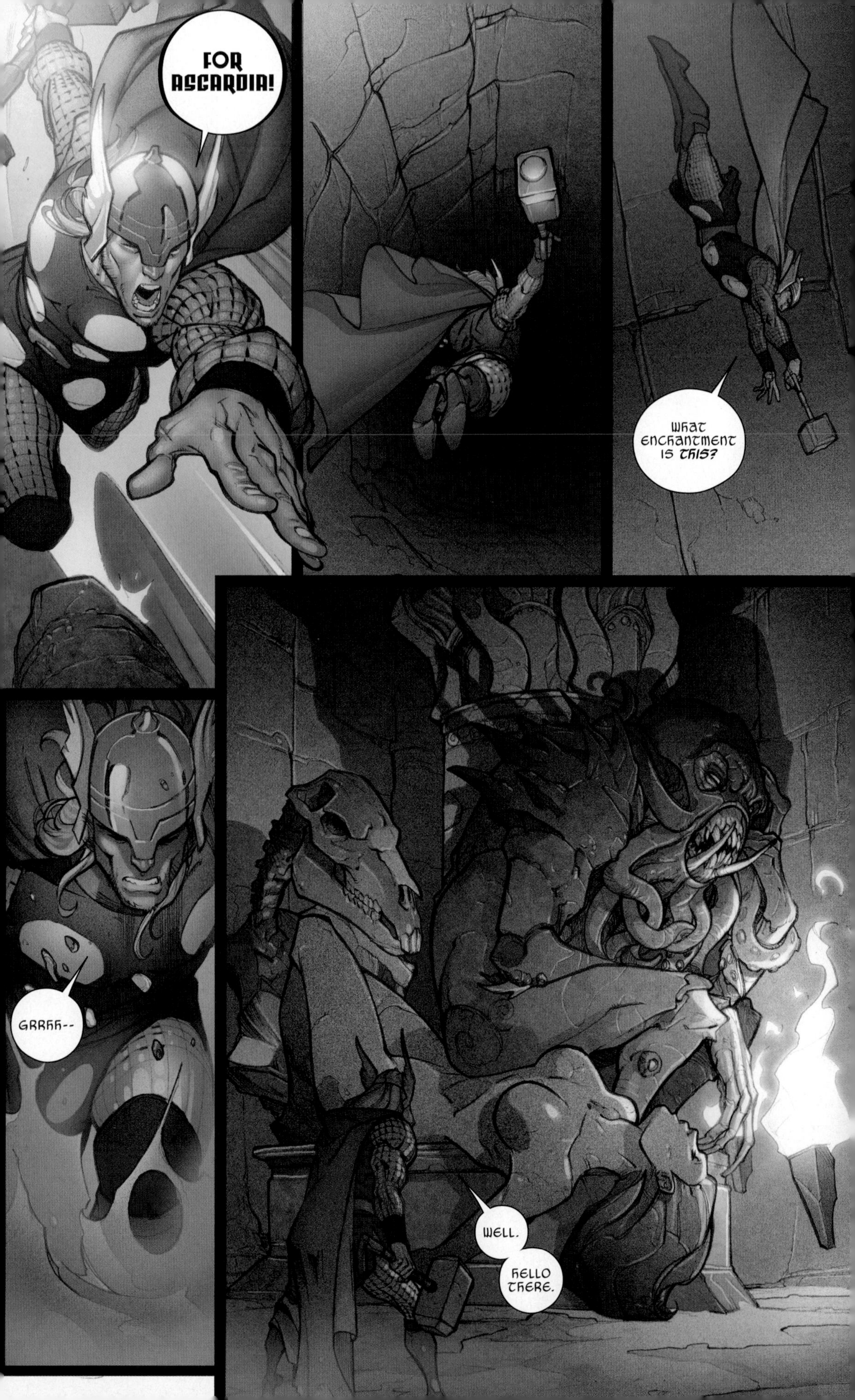

FOR ASGARDIA!
WHAT ENCHANTMENT IS THIS?
GRRHH--
WELL.
HELLO THERE.

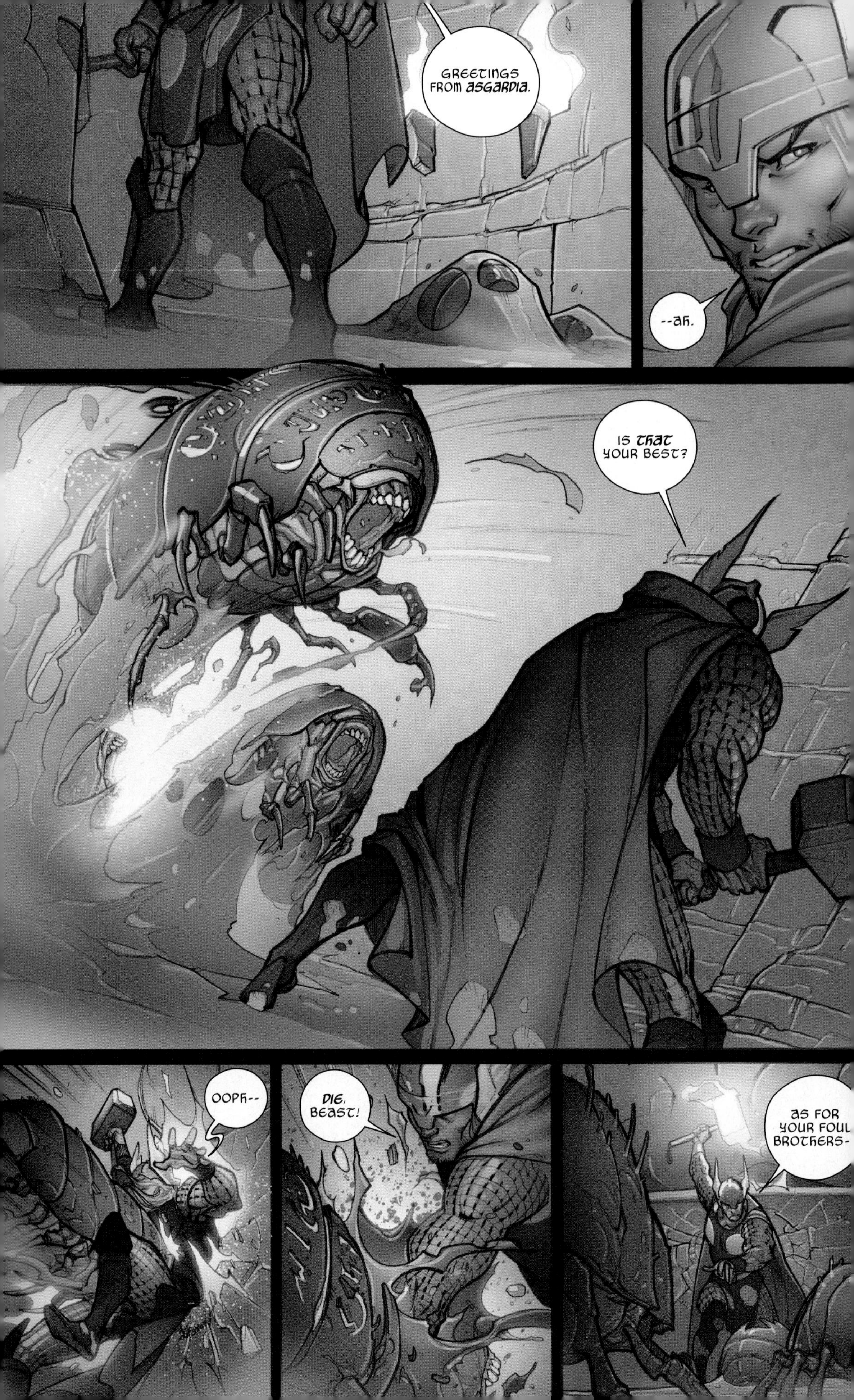
GREETINGS FROM *ASGARDIA.*
--AH.
IS *THAT* YOUR BEST?
OOPH--
DIE, BEAST!
AS FOR YOUR FOUL BROTHERS-

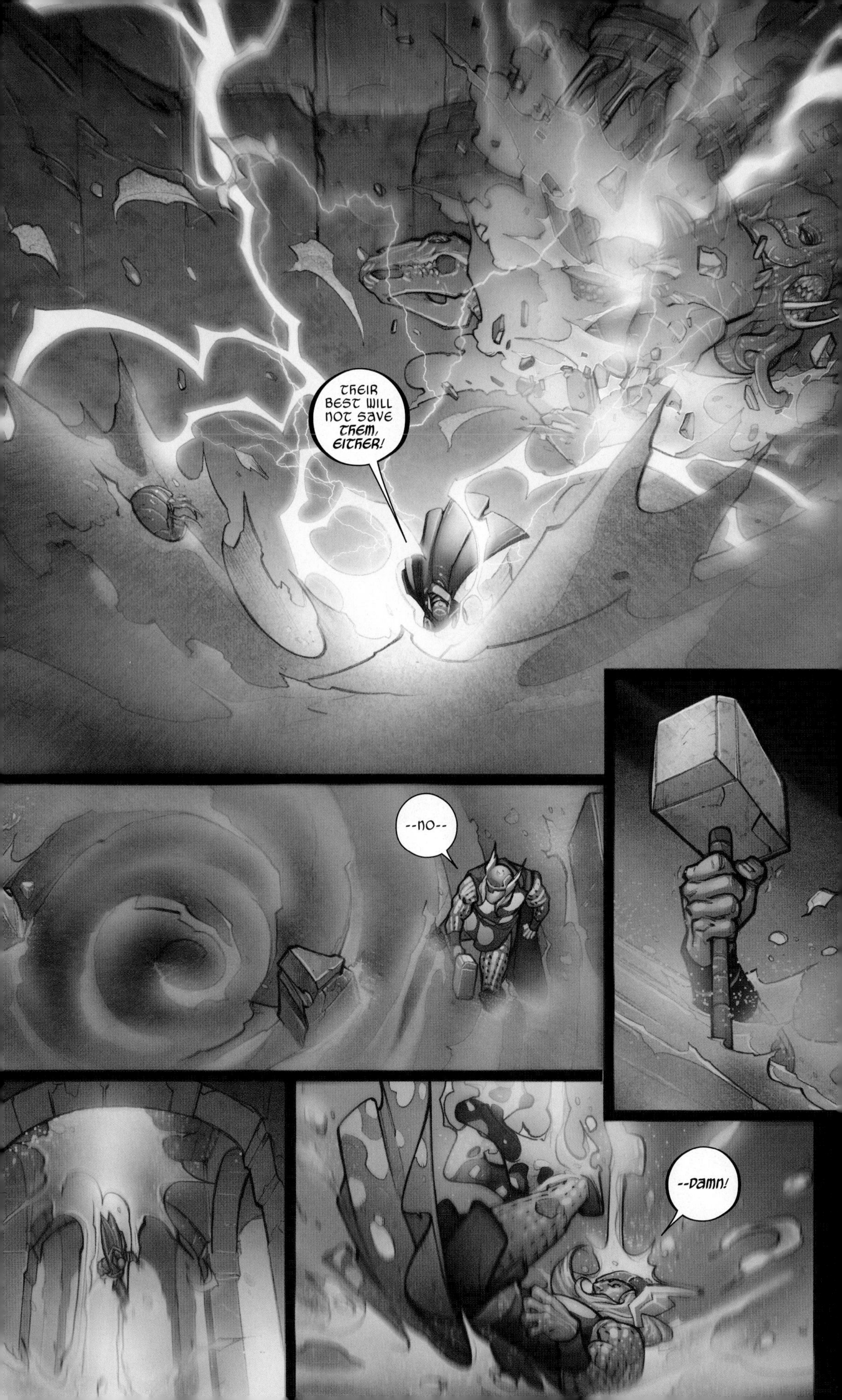
THEIR BEST WILL NOT SAVE THEM, EITHER!
--NO--
--DAMN!

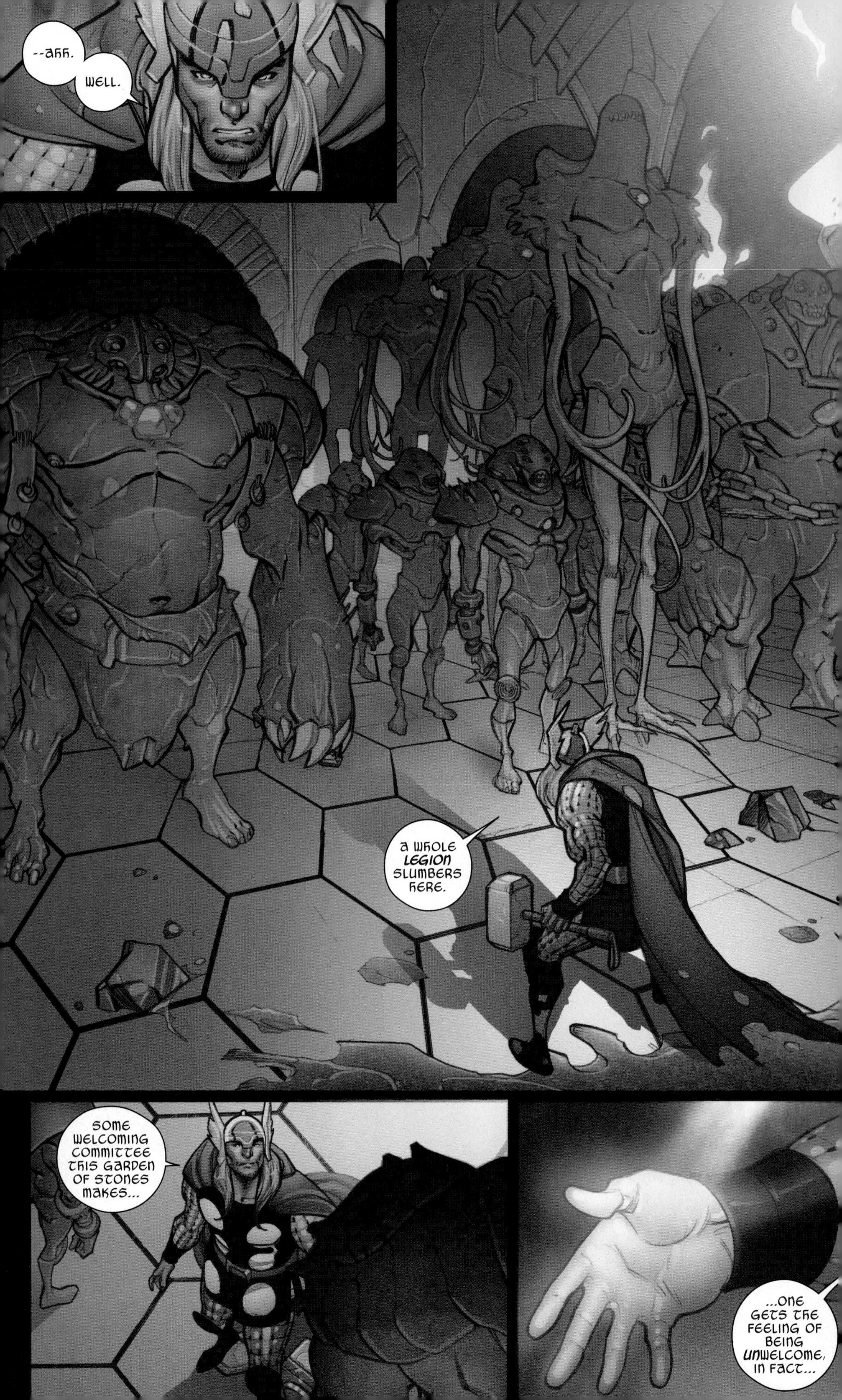
--AHH.
WELL.
A WHOLE LEGION SLUMBERS HERE.
SOME WELCOMING COMMITTEE THIS GARDEN OF STONES MAKES...
...ONE GETS THE FEELING OF BEING UNWELCOME, IN FACT...

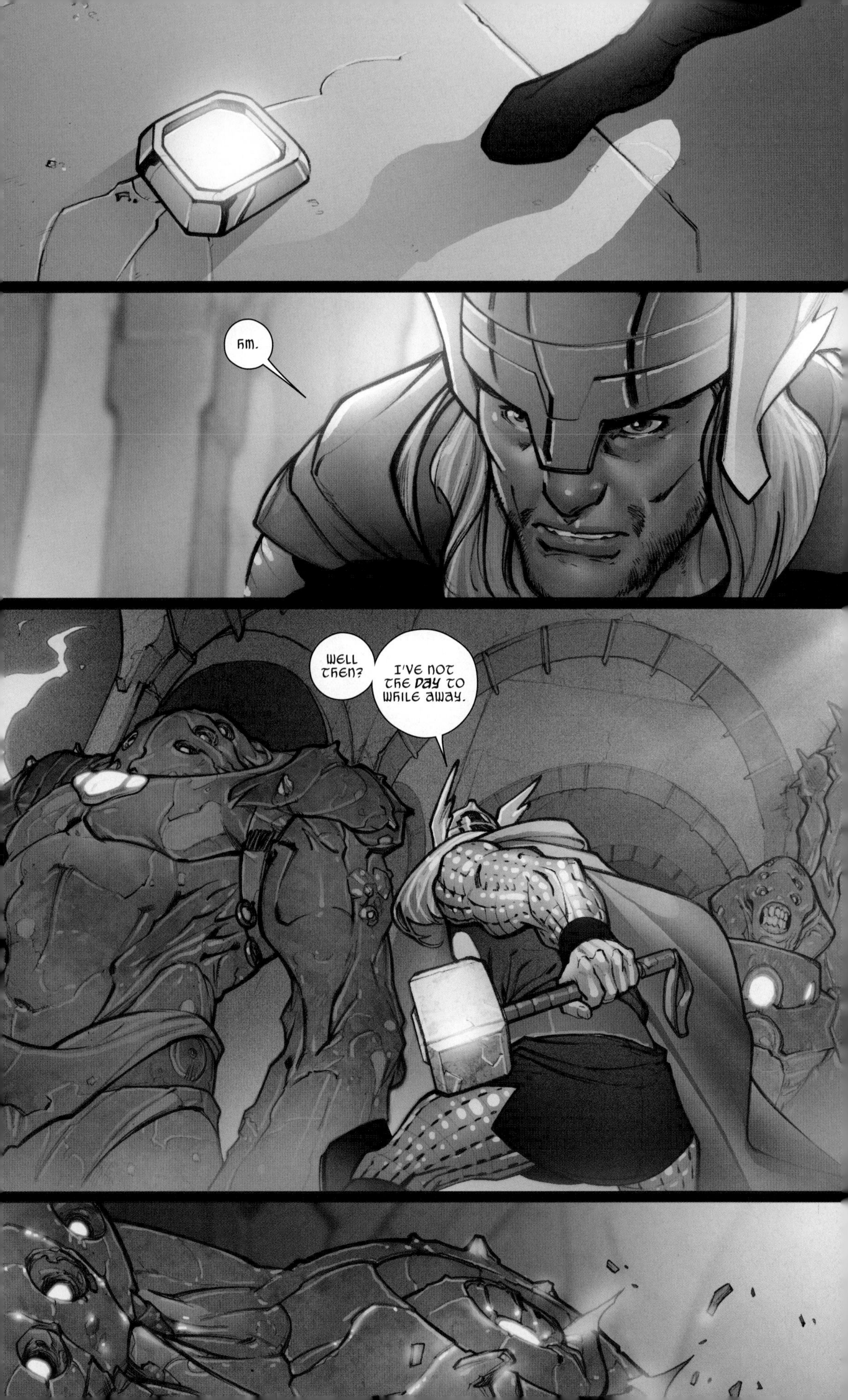
HM.
WELL THEN?
I'VE NOT THE DAY TO WHILE AWAY.

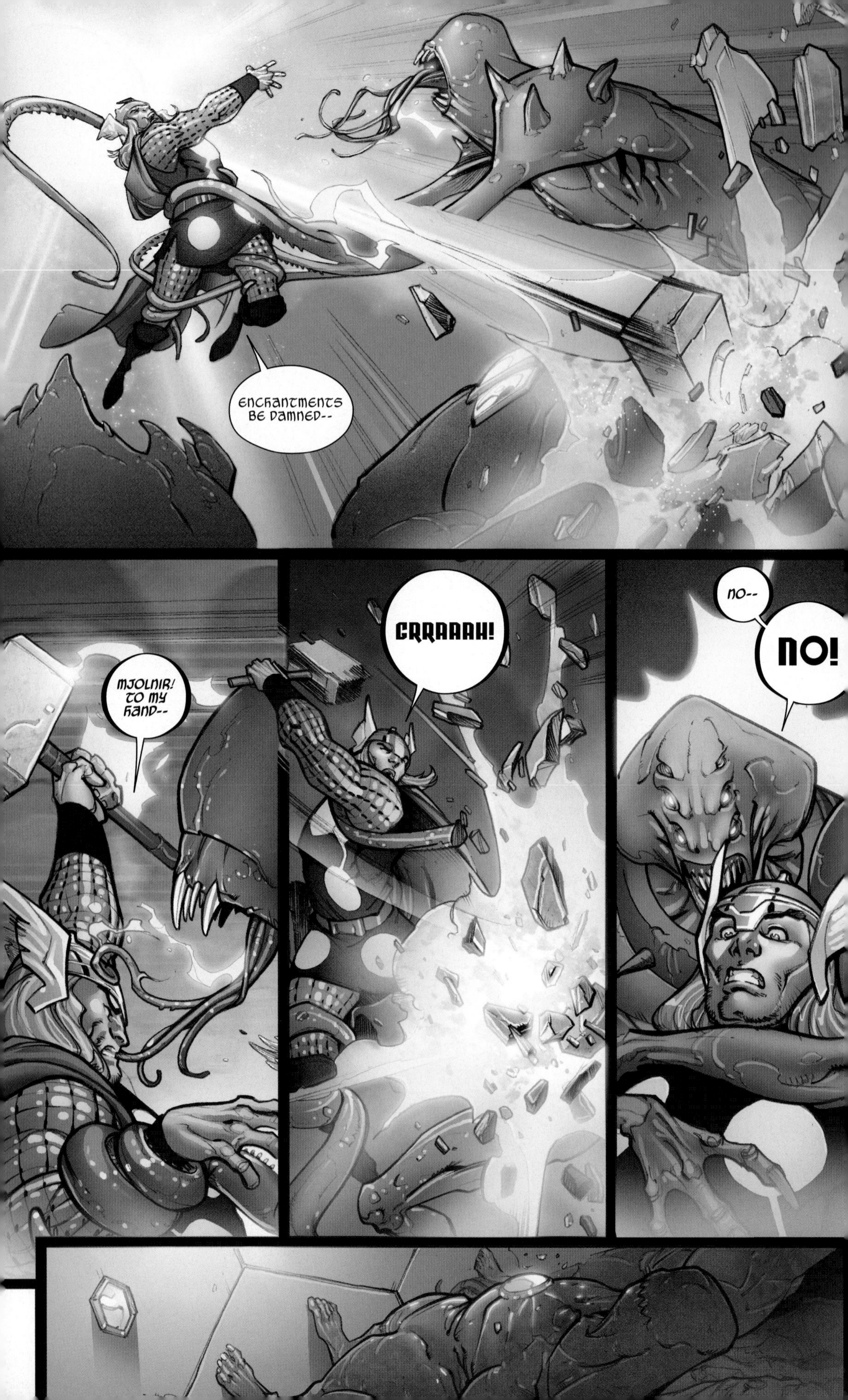
ENCHANTMENTS BE DAMNED--
MJOLNIR! TO MY HAND--
GRRAAAH!
NO--
NO!

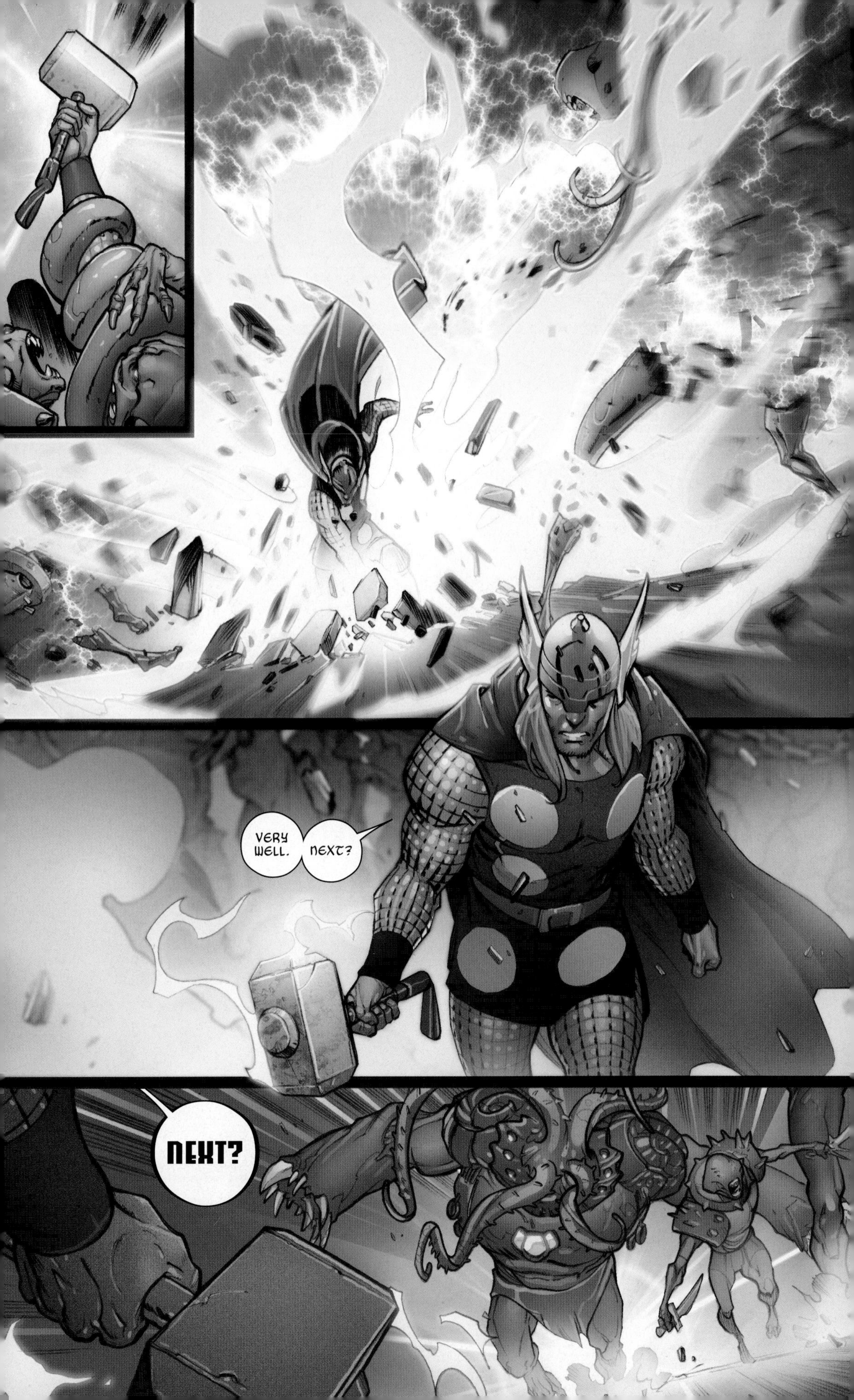

VERY WELL.
NEXT?
NEXT?

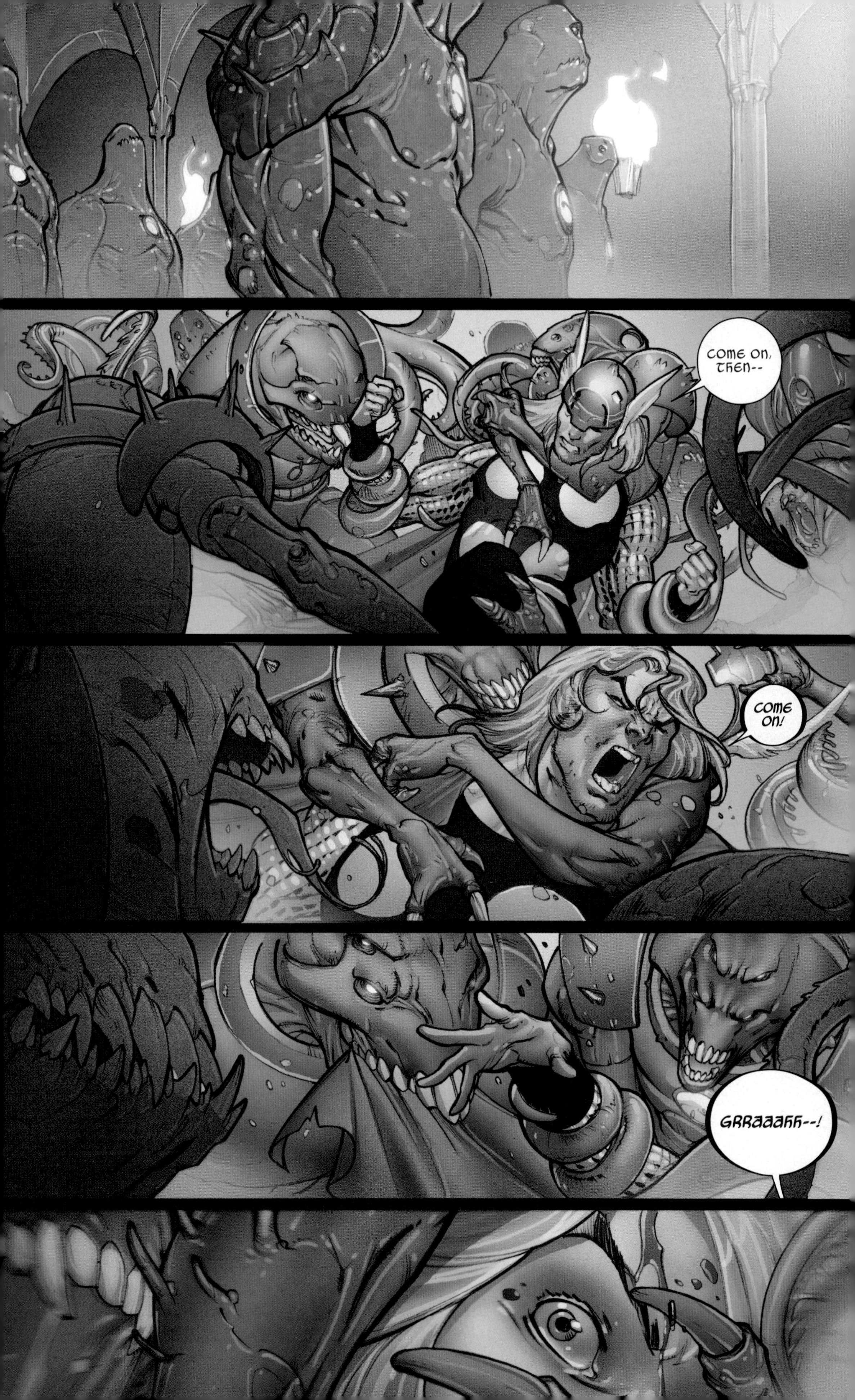
COME ON, THEN--
COME ON!
GRRAAAHH--!

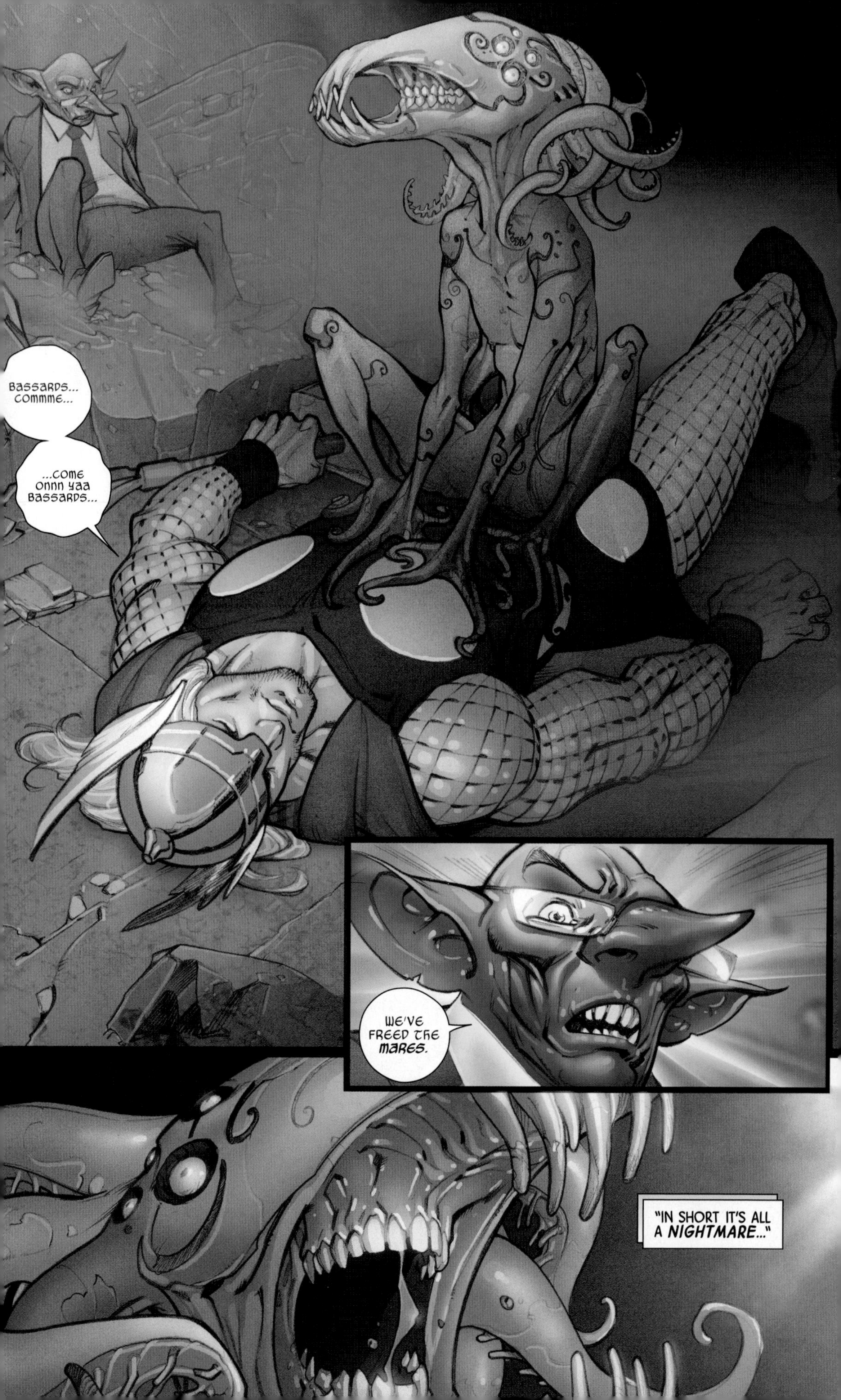
BASSARDS... COMMME...
...COME ONNN YAA BASSARDS...
WE'VE FREED THE MARES.
"IN SHORT IT'S ALL A NIGHTMARE..."

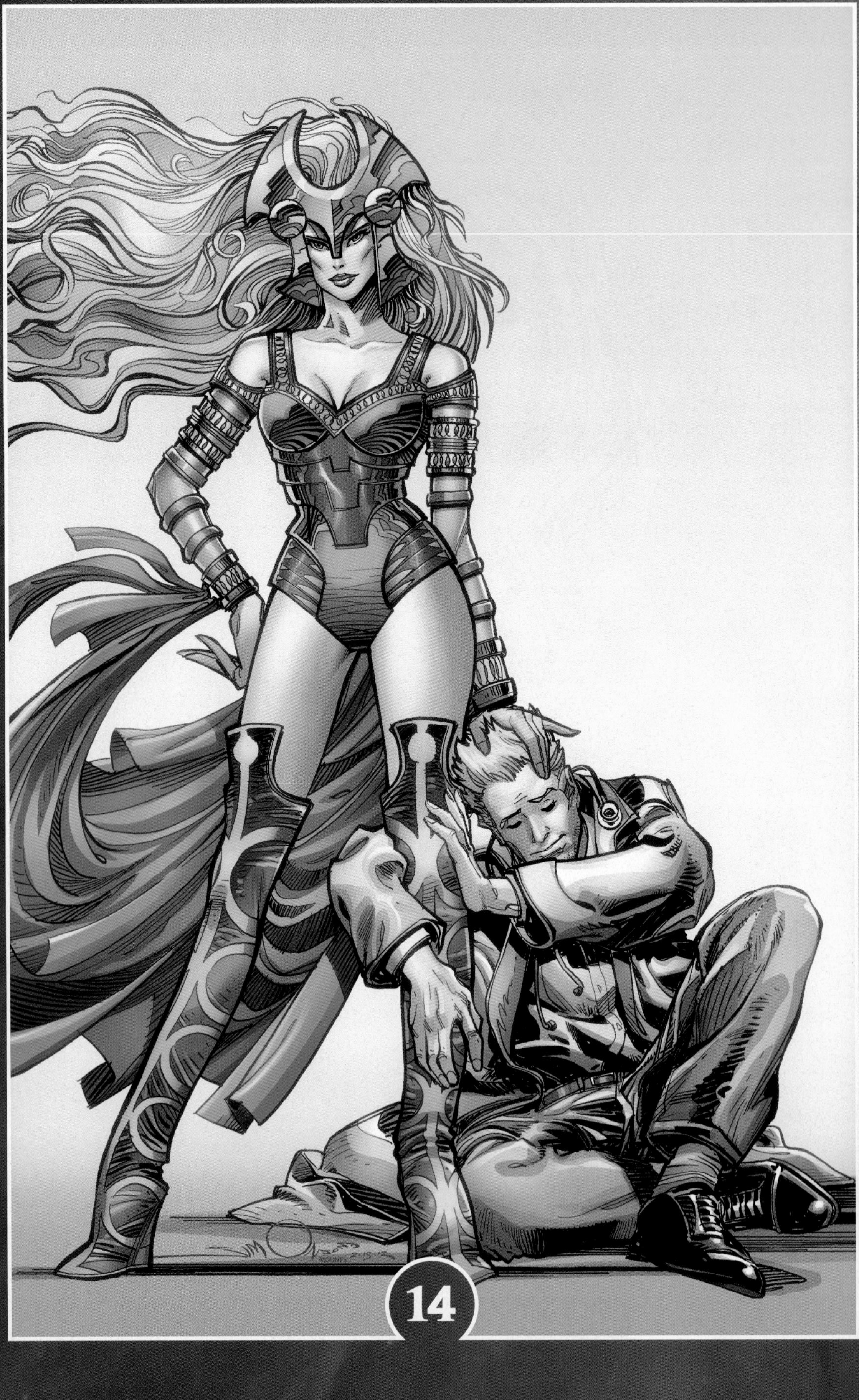

14

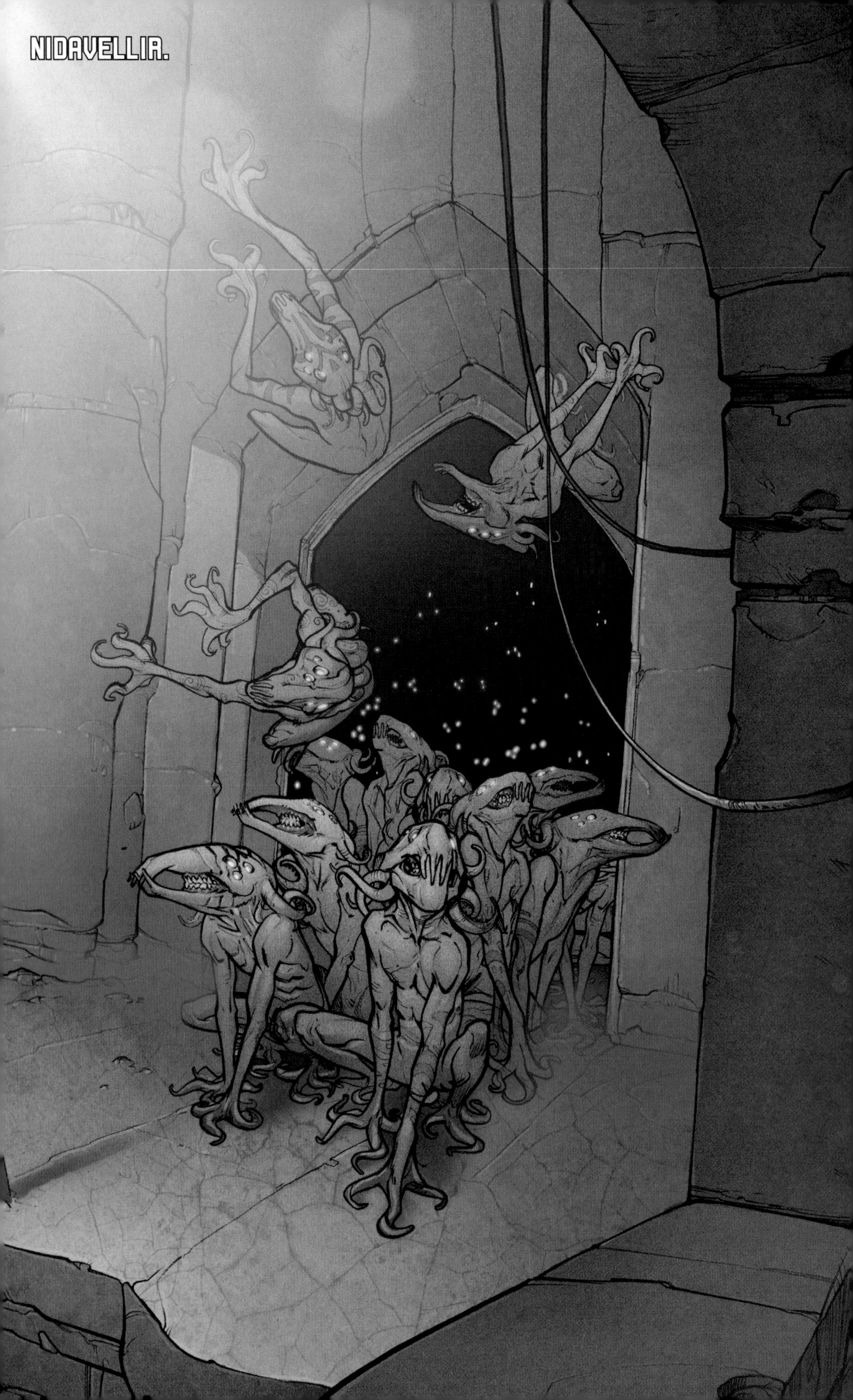
NIDAVELLIR.

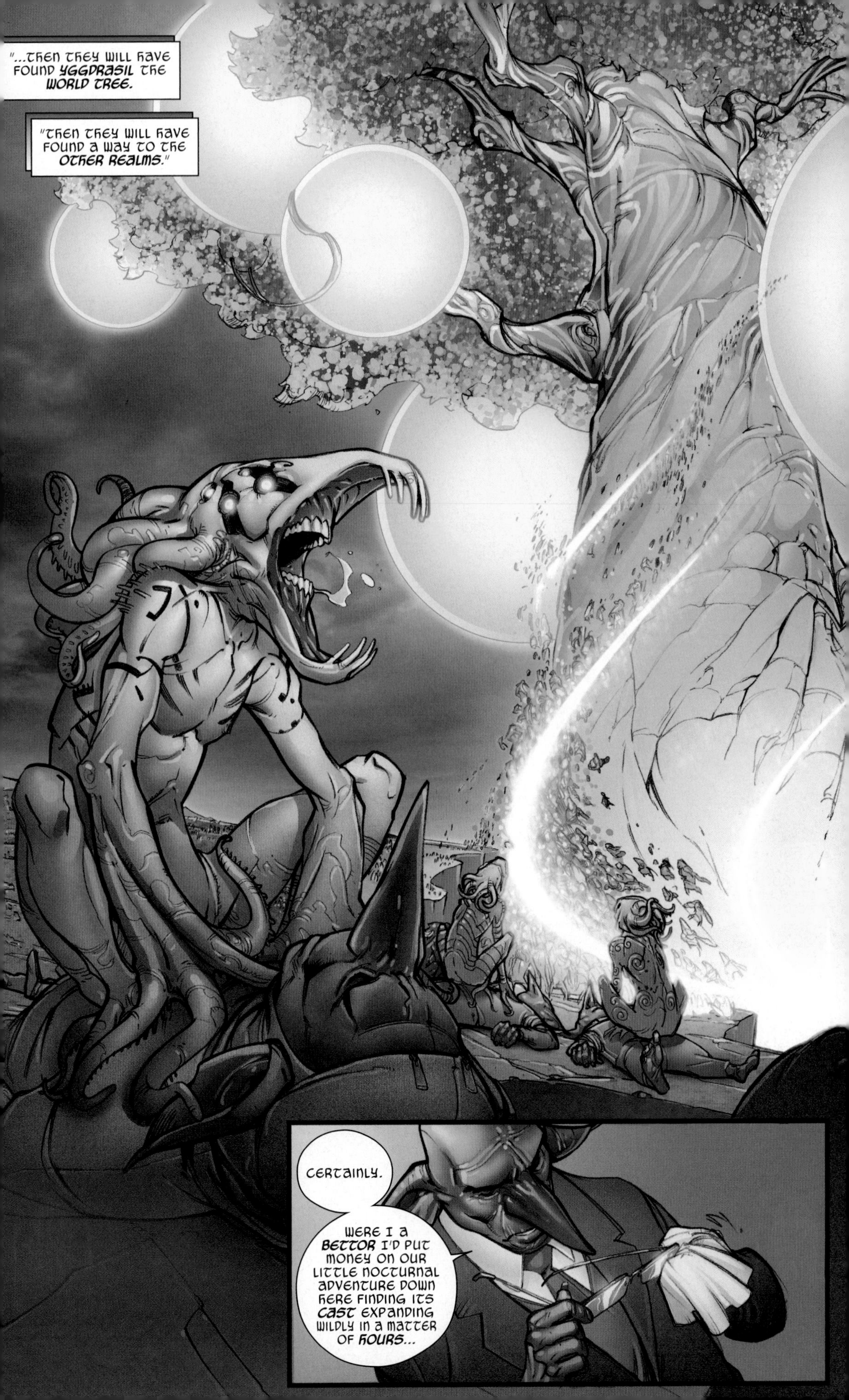
"...THEN THEY WILL HAVE FOUND YGGDRASIL THE WORLD TREE.
"THEN THEY WILL HAVE FOUND A WAY TO THE OTHER REALMS."
CERTAINLY.
WERE I A BETTOR I'D PUT MONEY ON OUR LITTLE NOCTURNAL ADVENTURE DOWN HERE FINDING ITS CAST EXPANDING WILDLY IN A MATTER OF HOURS...

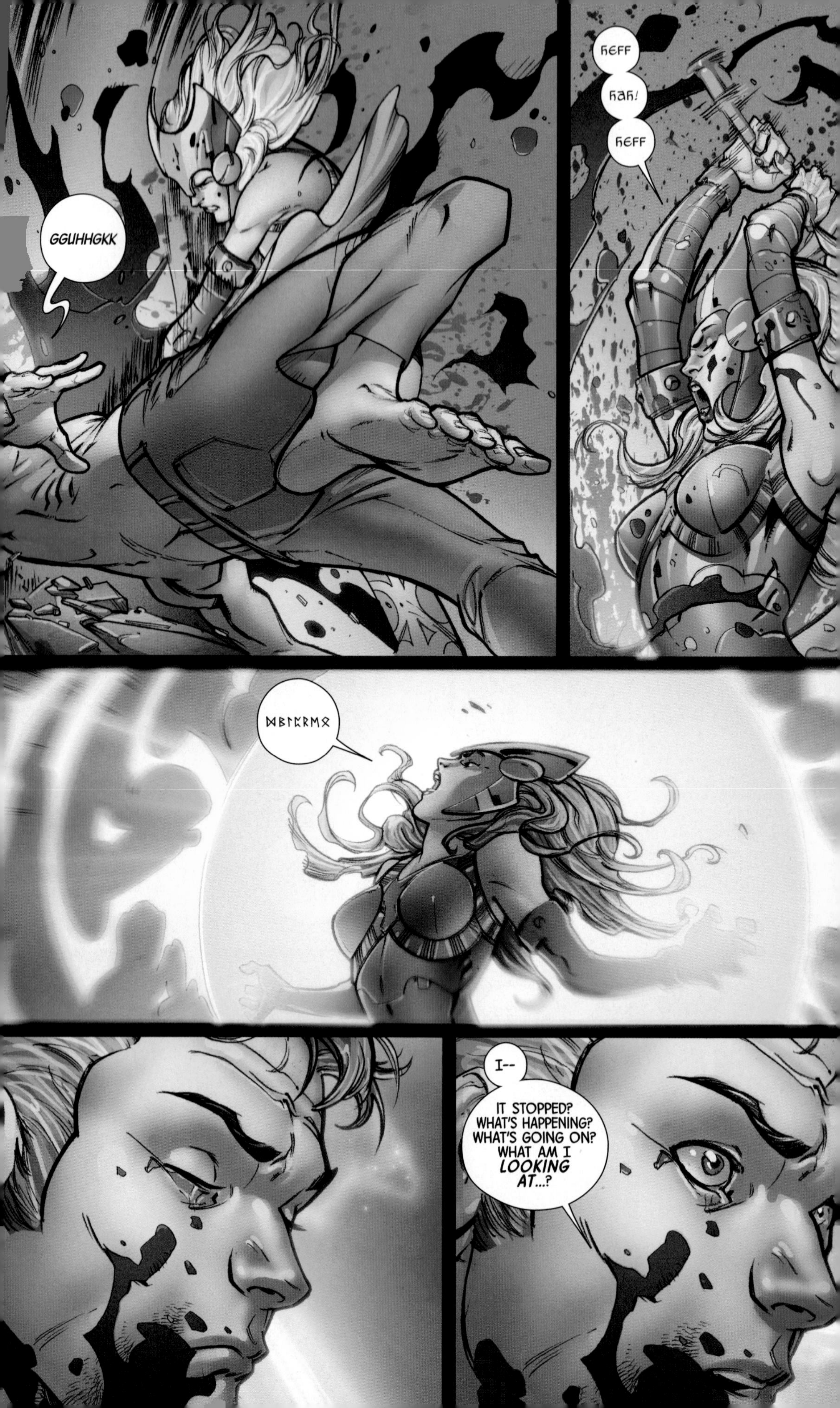
GGUHHGKK
HEFF
HAH!
HEFF
I--
IT STOPPED? WHAT'S HAPPENING? WHAT'S GOING ON? WHAT AM I *LOOKING* AT...?

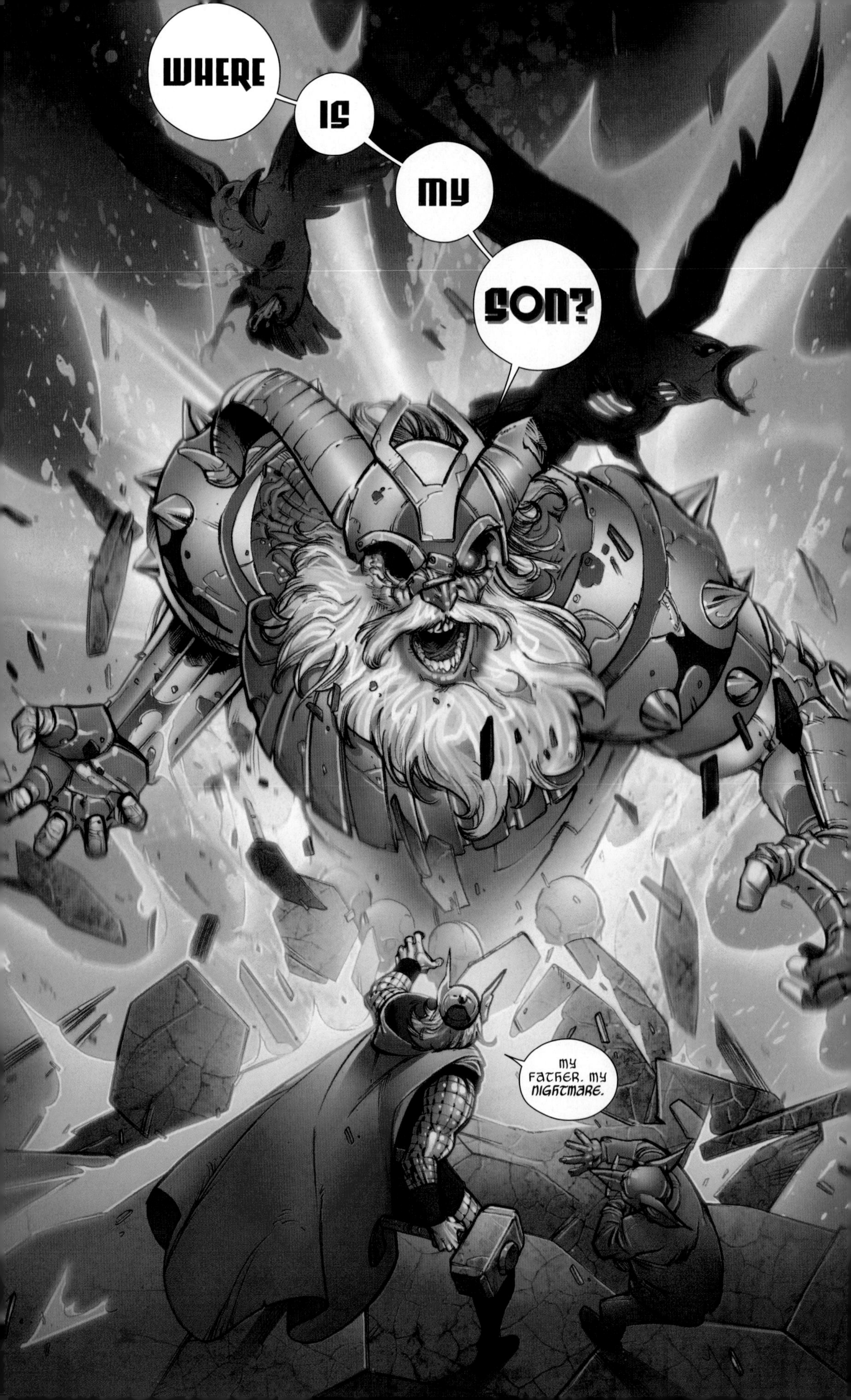
WHERE
IS
MY
SON?
MY FATHER. MY NIGHTMARE.

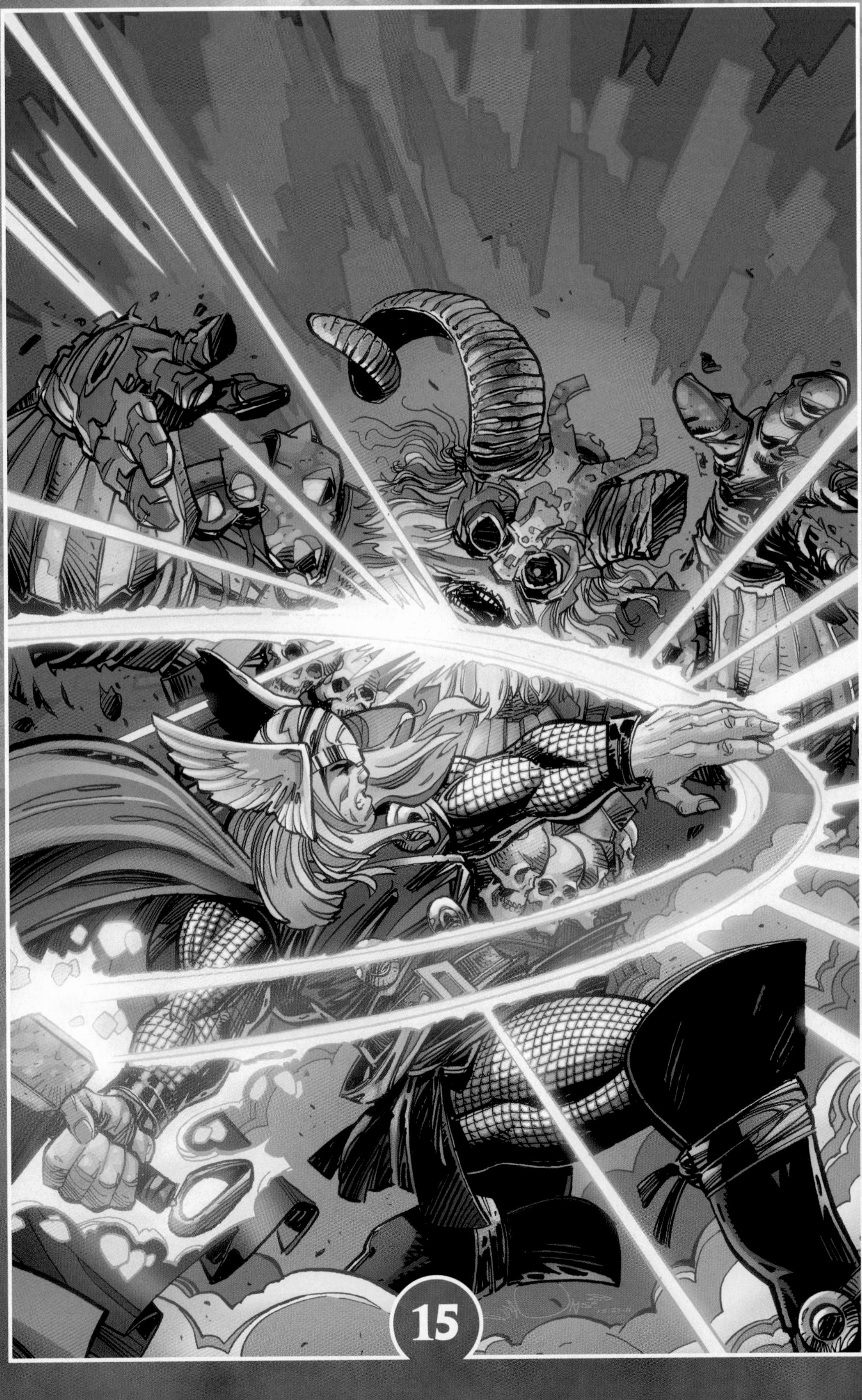

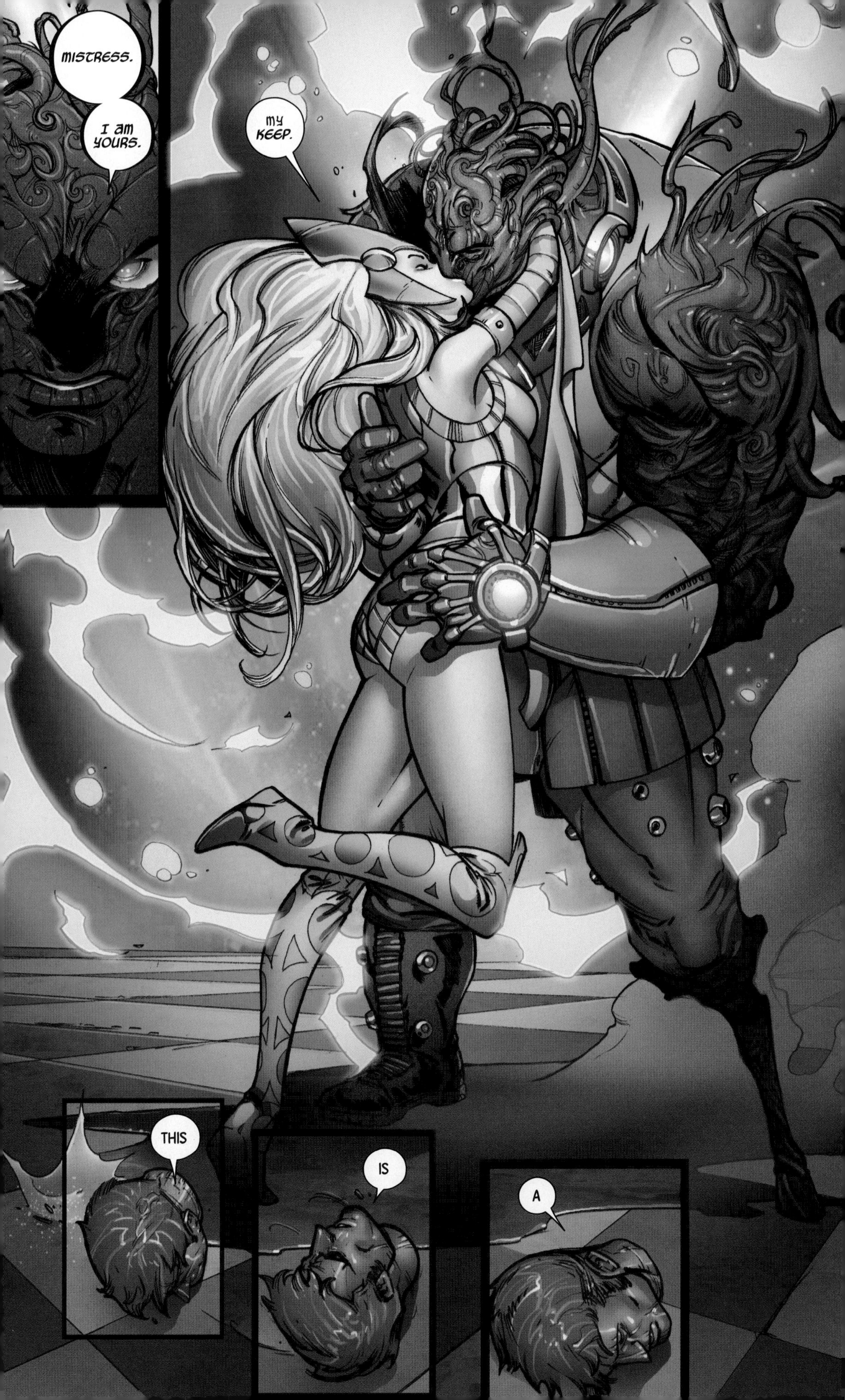
MISTRESS.
I AM YOURS.
MY KEEP.
THIS
IS
A

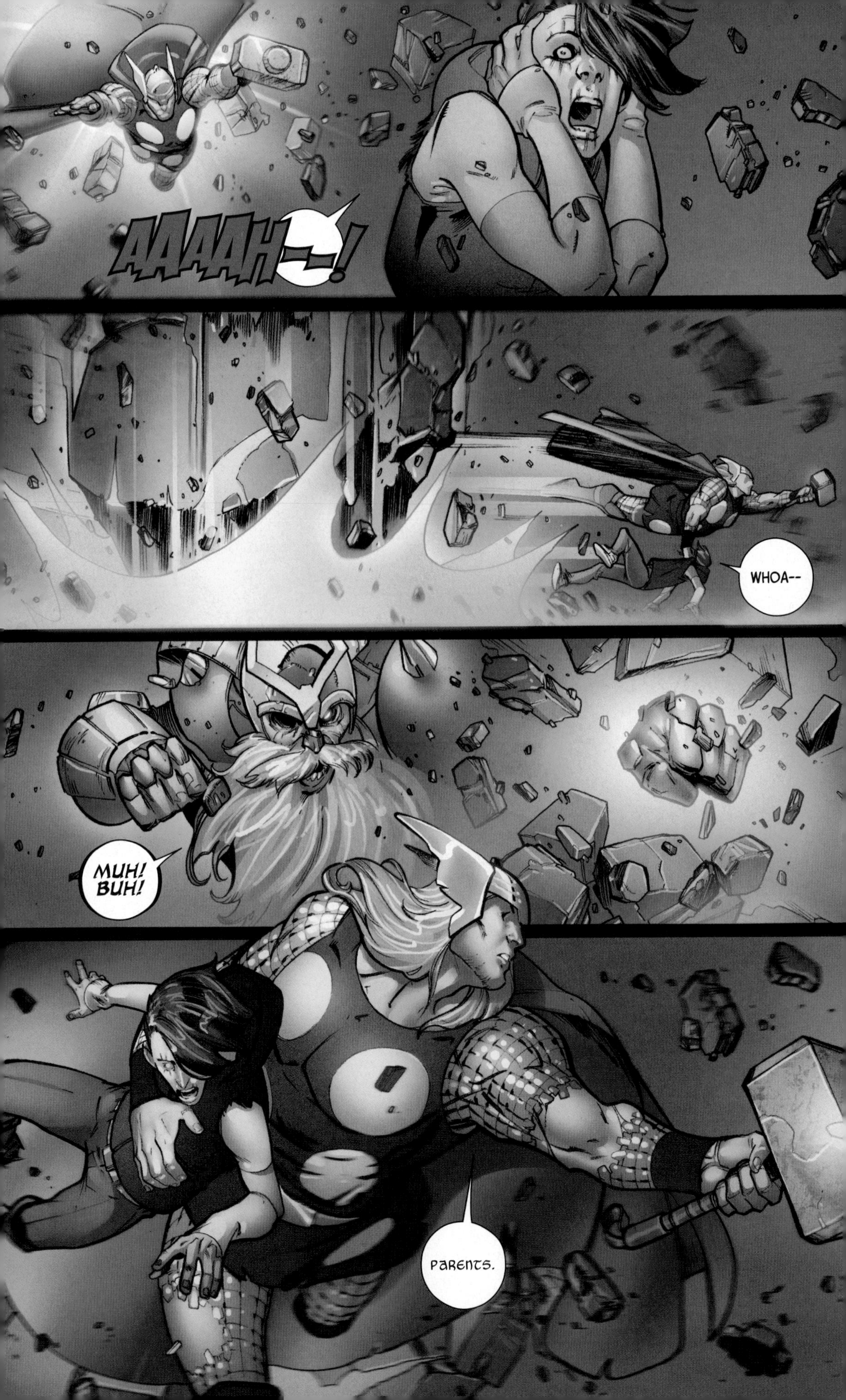
AAAAH--!
WHOA--
MUH! BUH!
PARENTS.

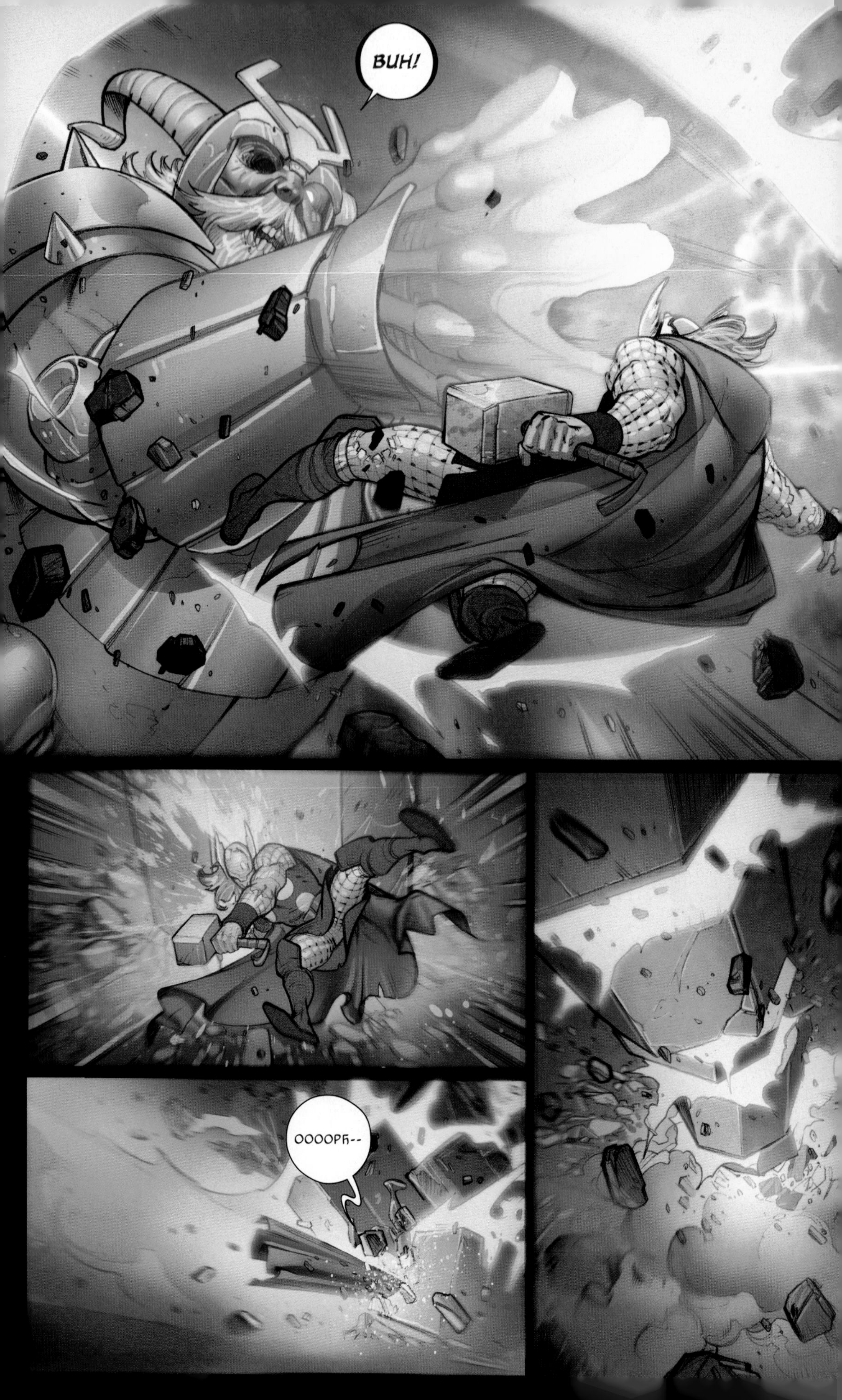
BUH!
OOOOPH--

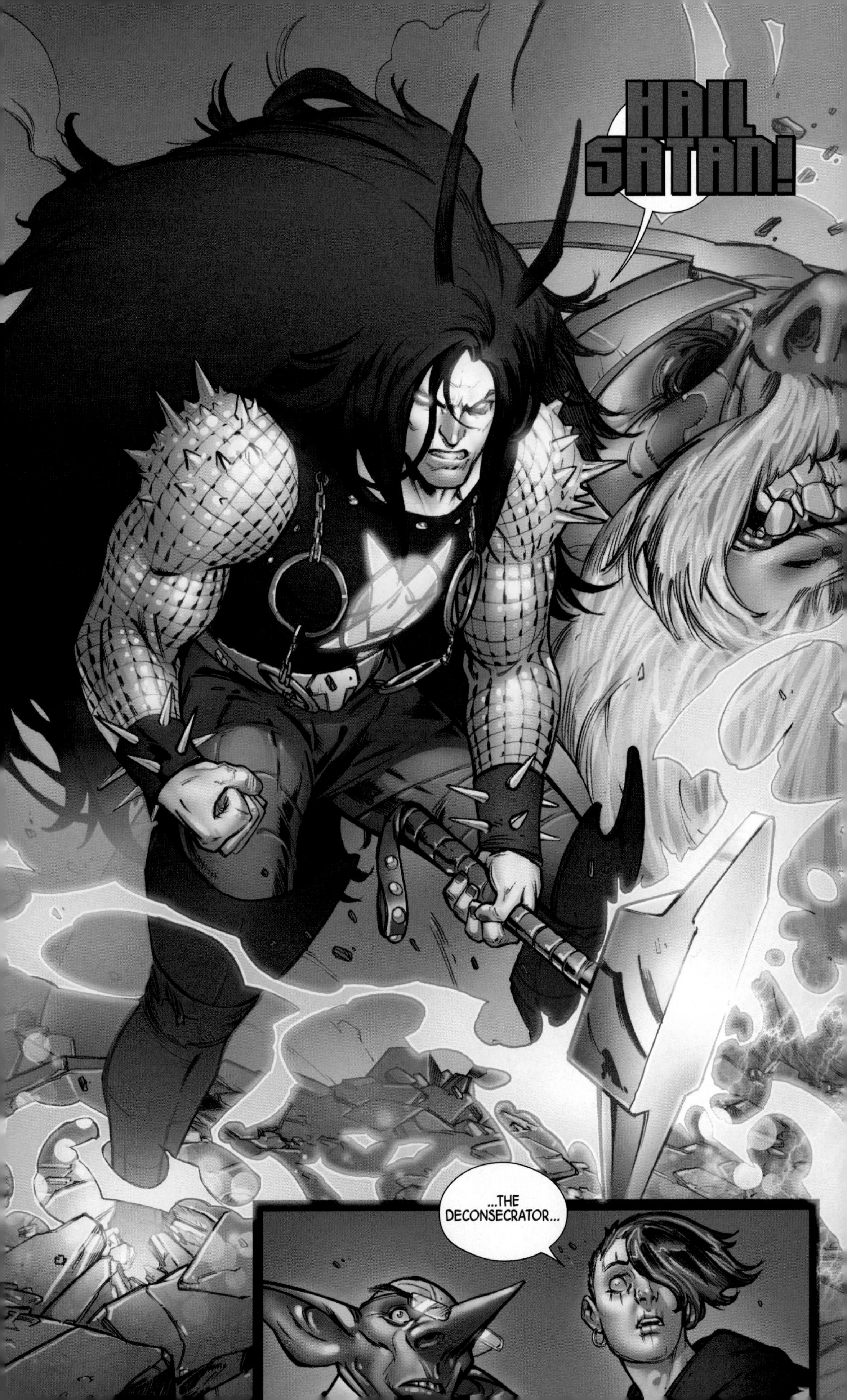
HAIL SATAN!
...THE DECONSECRATOR...

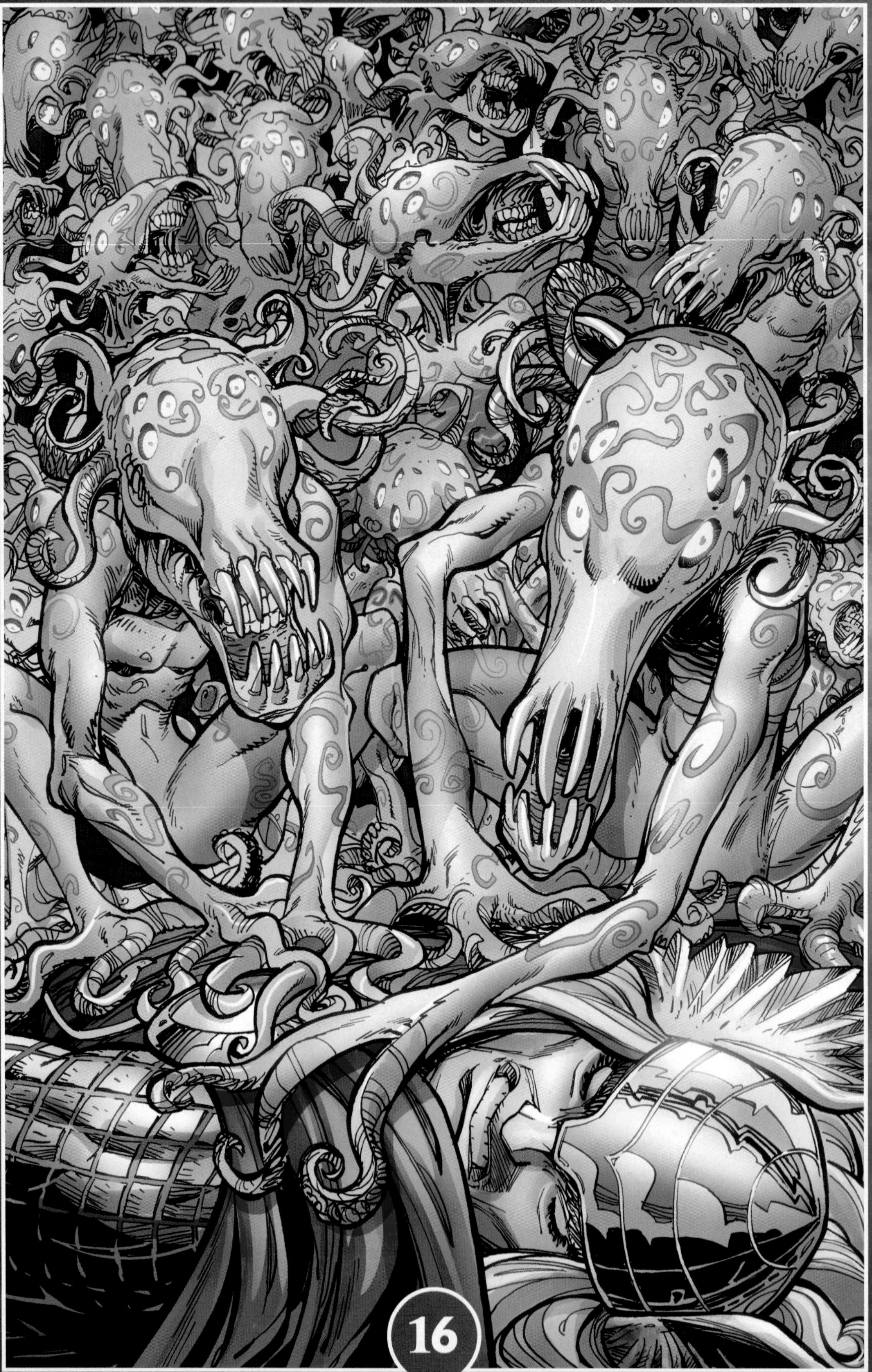

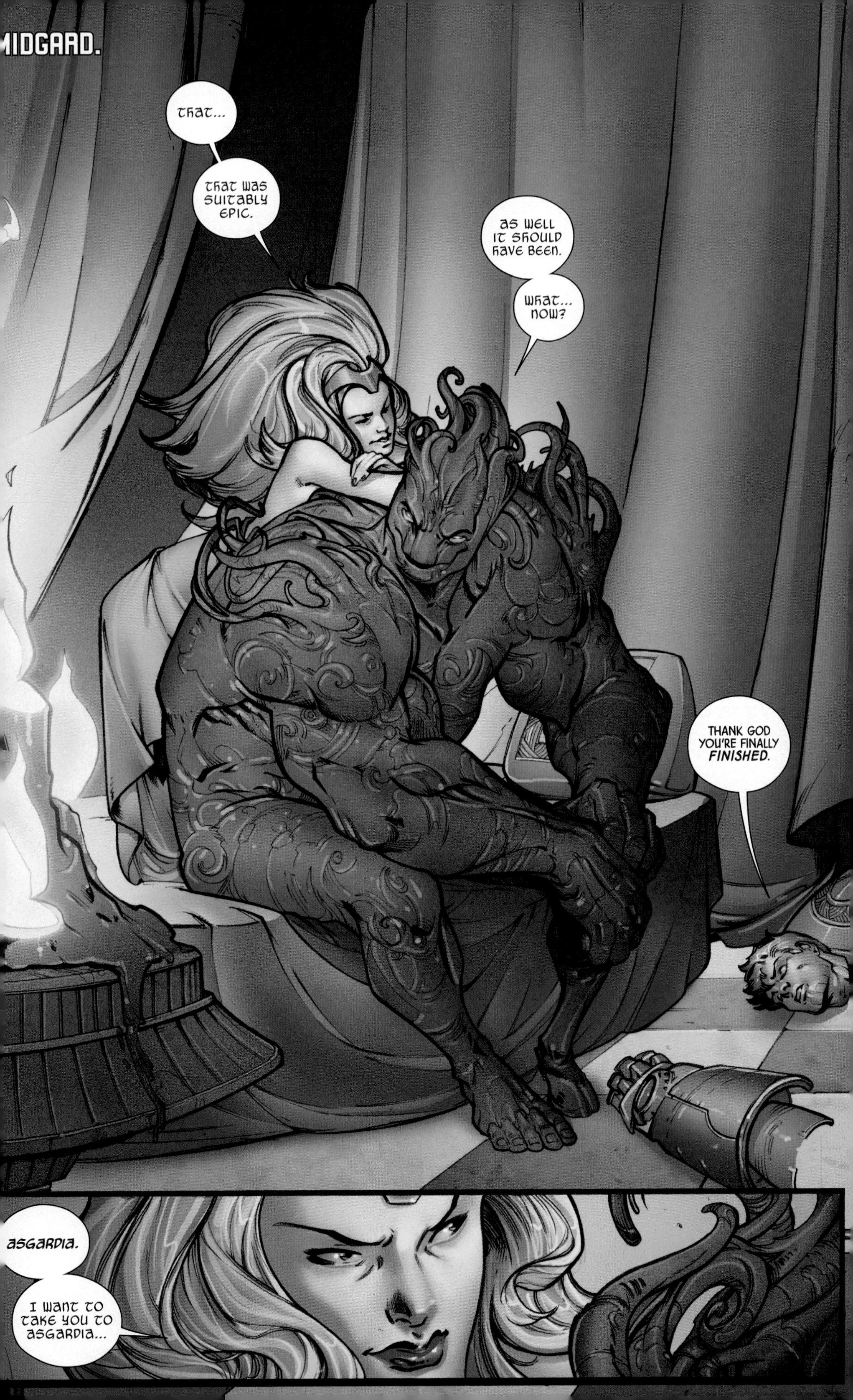
MIDGARD.
THAT...
THAT WAS SUITABLY EPIC.
AS WELL IT SHOULD HAVE BEEN.
WHAT... NOW?
THANK GOD YOU'RE FINALLY *FINISHED*.
ASGARDIA.
I WANT TO TAKE YOU TO ASGARDIA...

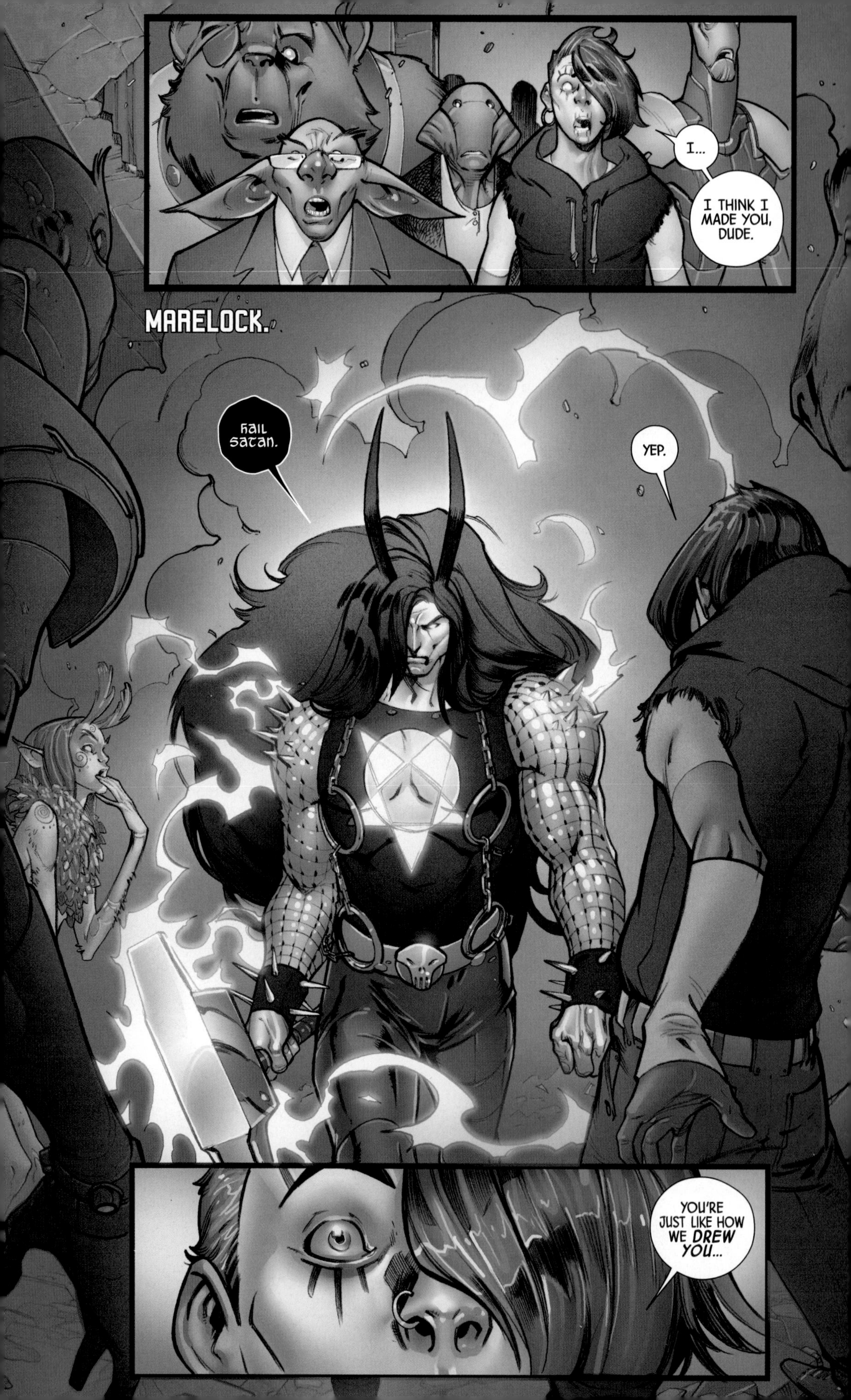
I...
I THINK I MADE YOU, DUDE.
MARELOCK.
hail satan.
YEP.
YOU'RE JUST LIKE HOW WE *DREW YOU*...

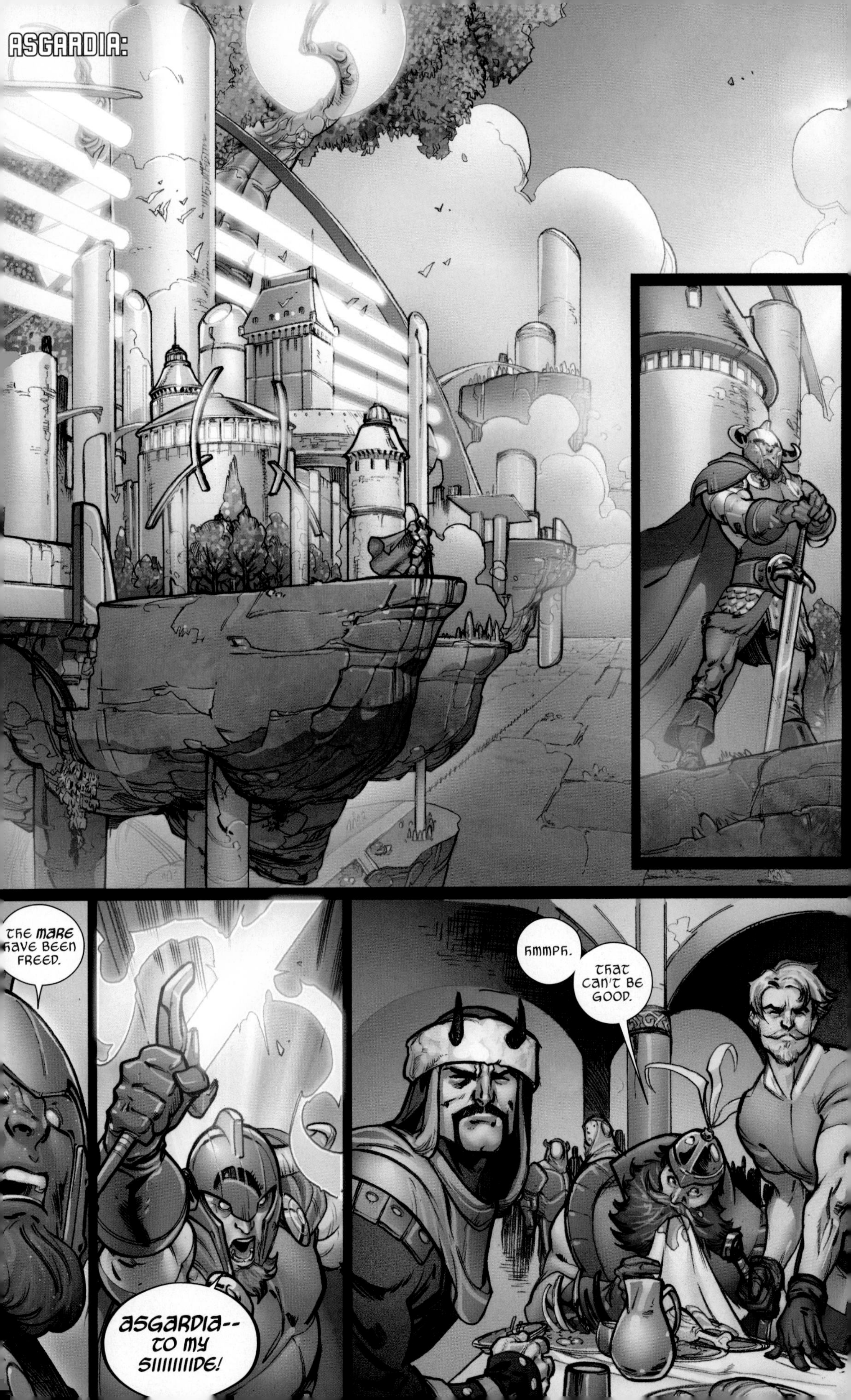
ASGARDIA:
THE MARE HAVE BEEN FREED.
ASGARDIA-- TO MY SIIIIIIIDE!
HMMPH.
THAT CAN'T BE GOOD.

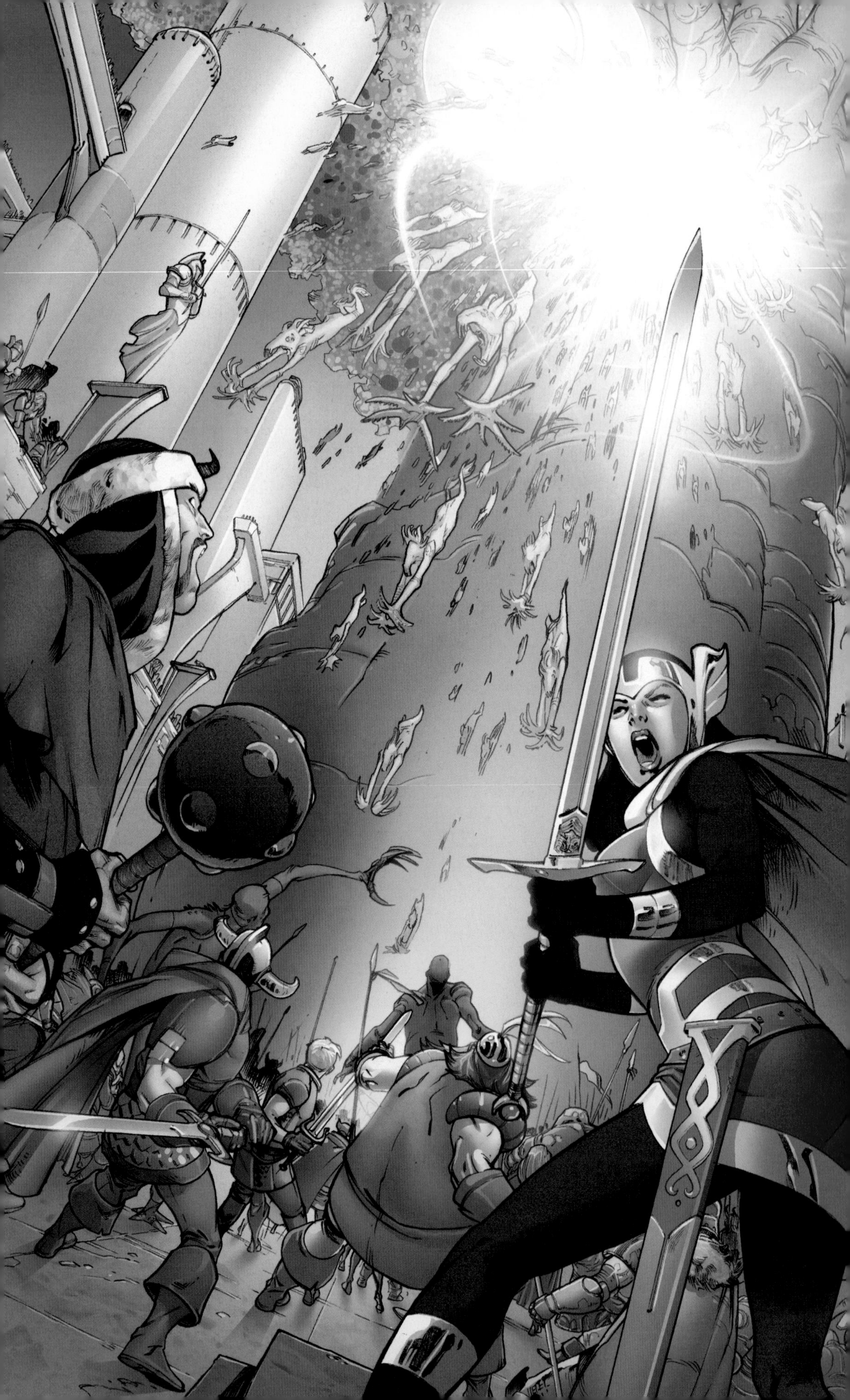

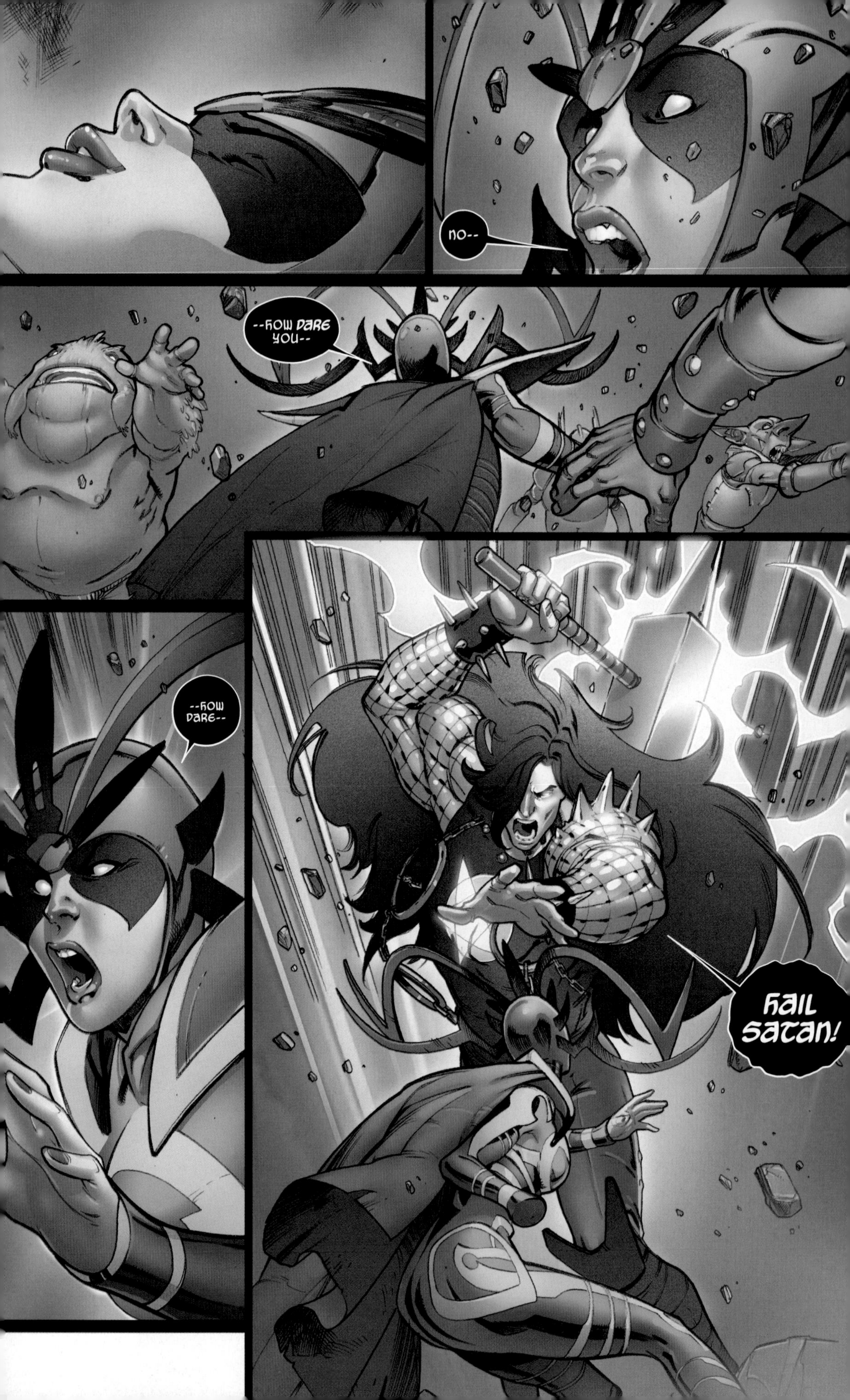
no--
--how dare you--
--how dare--
hail satan!

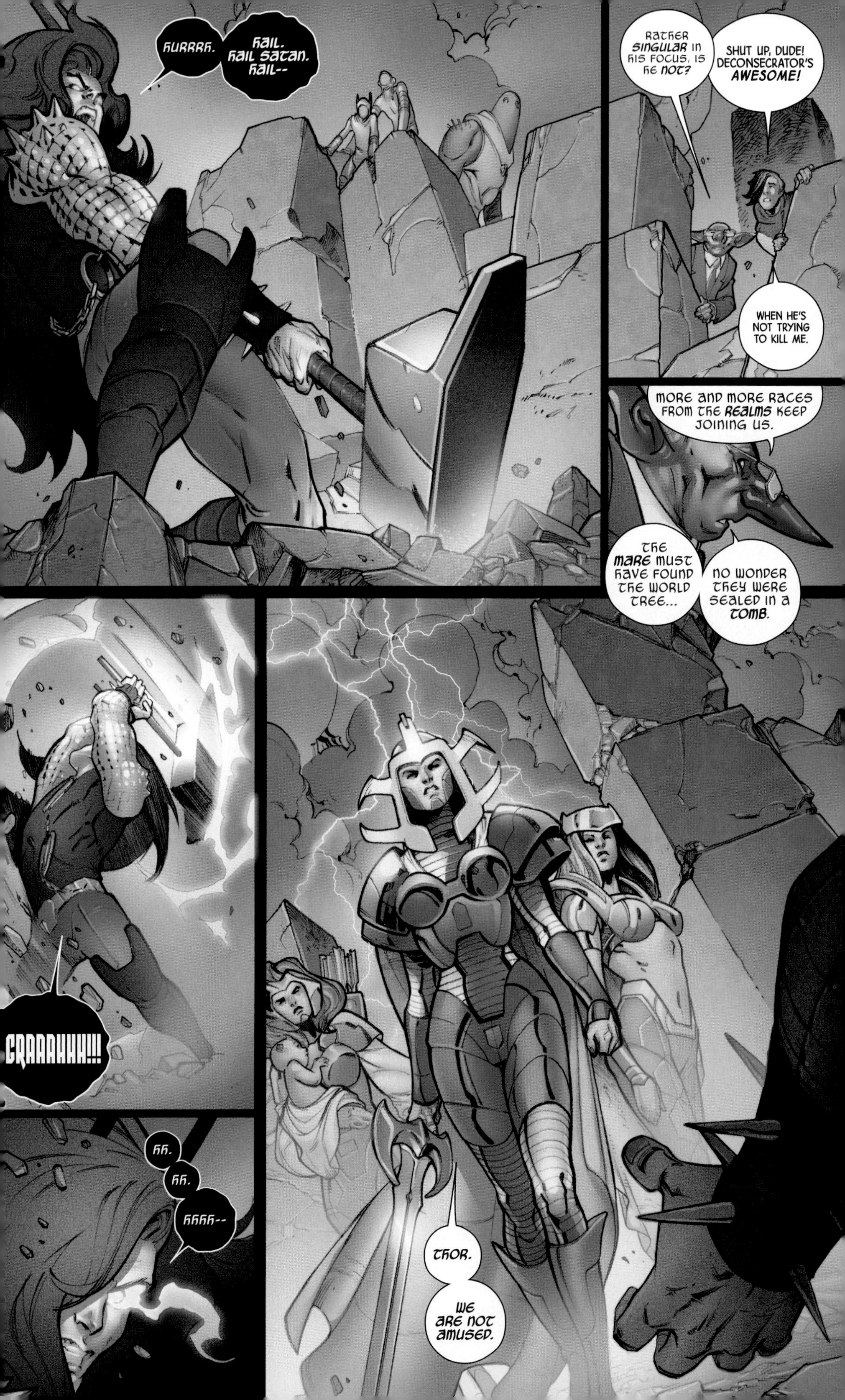
HURRRH.
HAIL. HAIL SATAN. HAIL--
RATHER SINGULAR IN HIS FOCUS, IS HE NOT?
SHUT UP, DUDE! DECONSECRATOR'S AWESOME!
WHEN HE'S NOT TRYING TO KILL ME.
MORE AND MORE RACES FROM THE REALMS KEEP JOINING US.
THE MARE MUST HAVE FOUND THE WORLD TREE...
NO WONDER THEY WERE SEALED IN A TOMB.
GRAAAHHH!!!
HH.
HH.
HHHH--
THOR.
WE ARE NOT AMUSED.

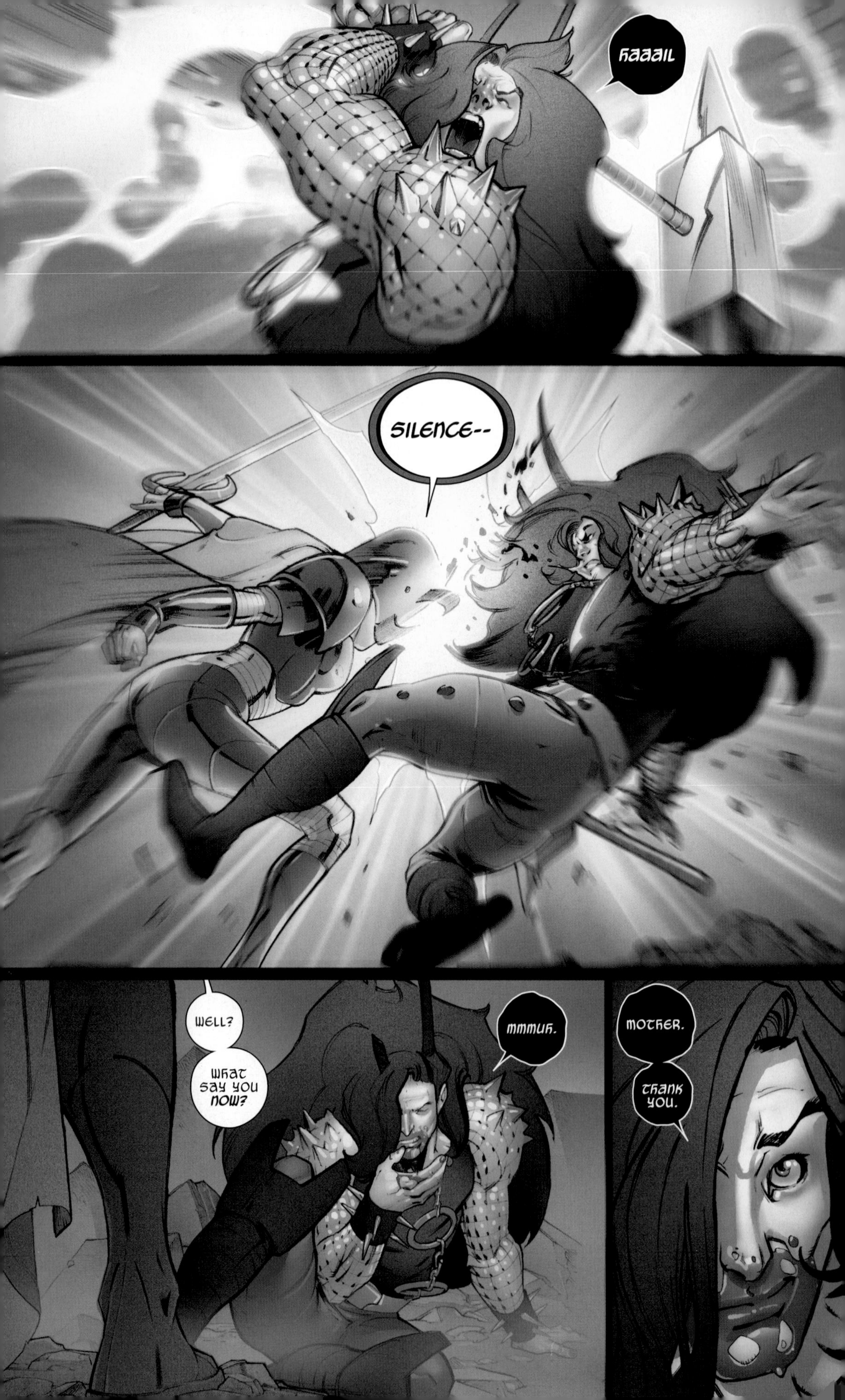
HAAAIL
SILENCE--
WELL?
WHAT SAY YOU NOW?
MMMUH.
MOTHER.
THANK YOU.

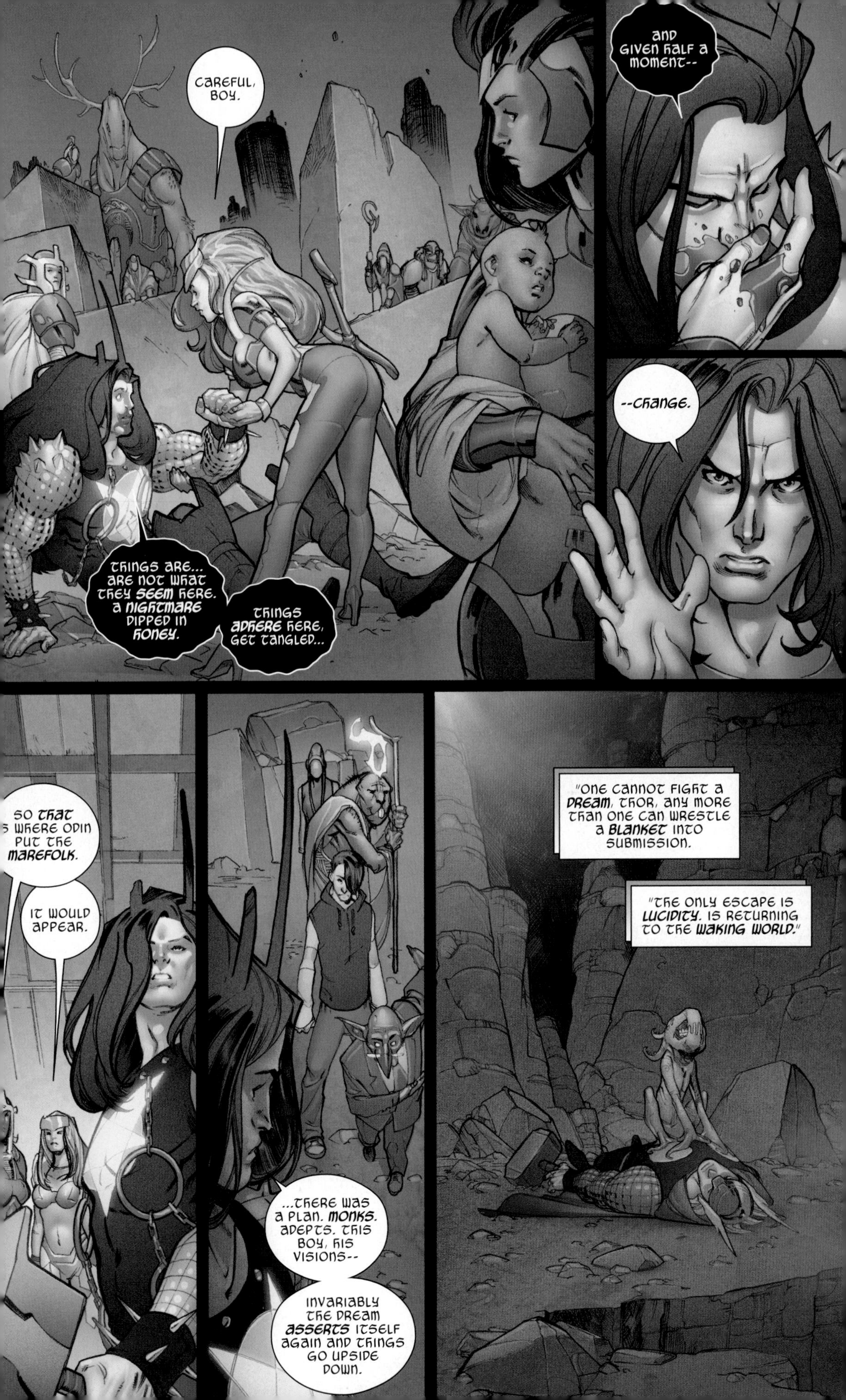
CAREFUL, BOY.
THINGS ARE... ARE NOT WHAT THEY SEEM HERE. A NIGHTMARE DIPPED IN HONEY.
THINGS ADHERE HERE, GET TANGLED...
AND GIVEN HALF A MOMENT--
--CHANGE.
SO THAT 'S WHERE ODIN PUT THE MAREFOLK.
IT WOULD APPEAR.
...THERE WAS A PLAN. MONKS. ADEPTS. THIS BOY, HIS VISIONS--
INVARIABLY THE DREAM ASSERTS ITSELF AGAIN AND THINGS GO UPSIDE DOWN.
"ONE CANNOT FIGHT A DREAM, THOR, ANY MORE THAN ONE CAN WRESTLE A BLANKET INTO SUBMISSION.
"THE ONLY ESCAPE IS LUCIDITY. IS RETURNING TO THE WAKING WORLD."

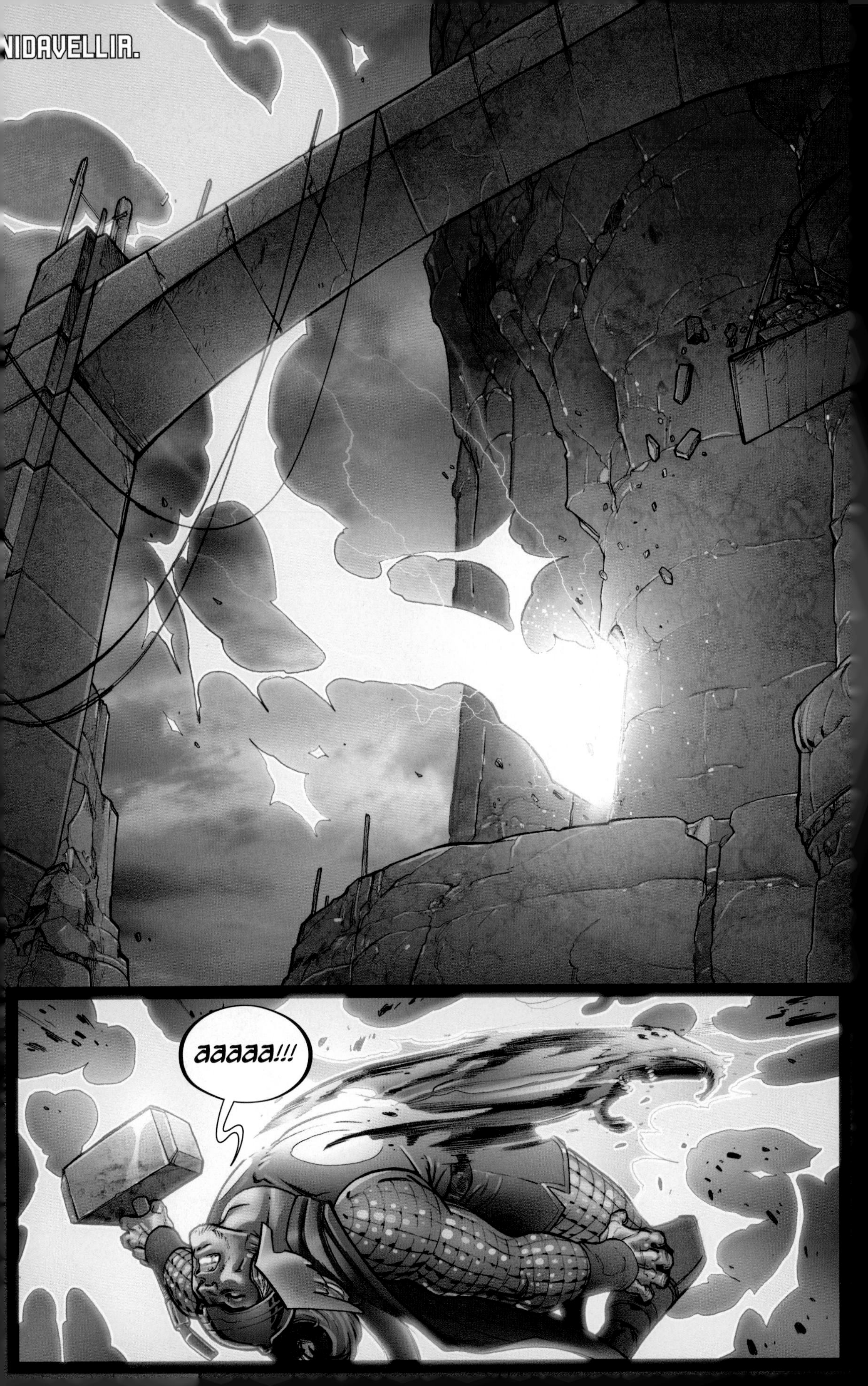
NIDAVELLIR.
aaaaa!!!

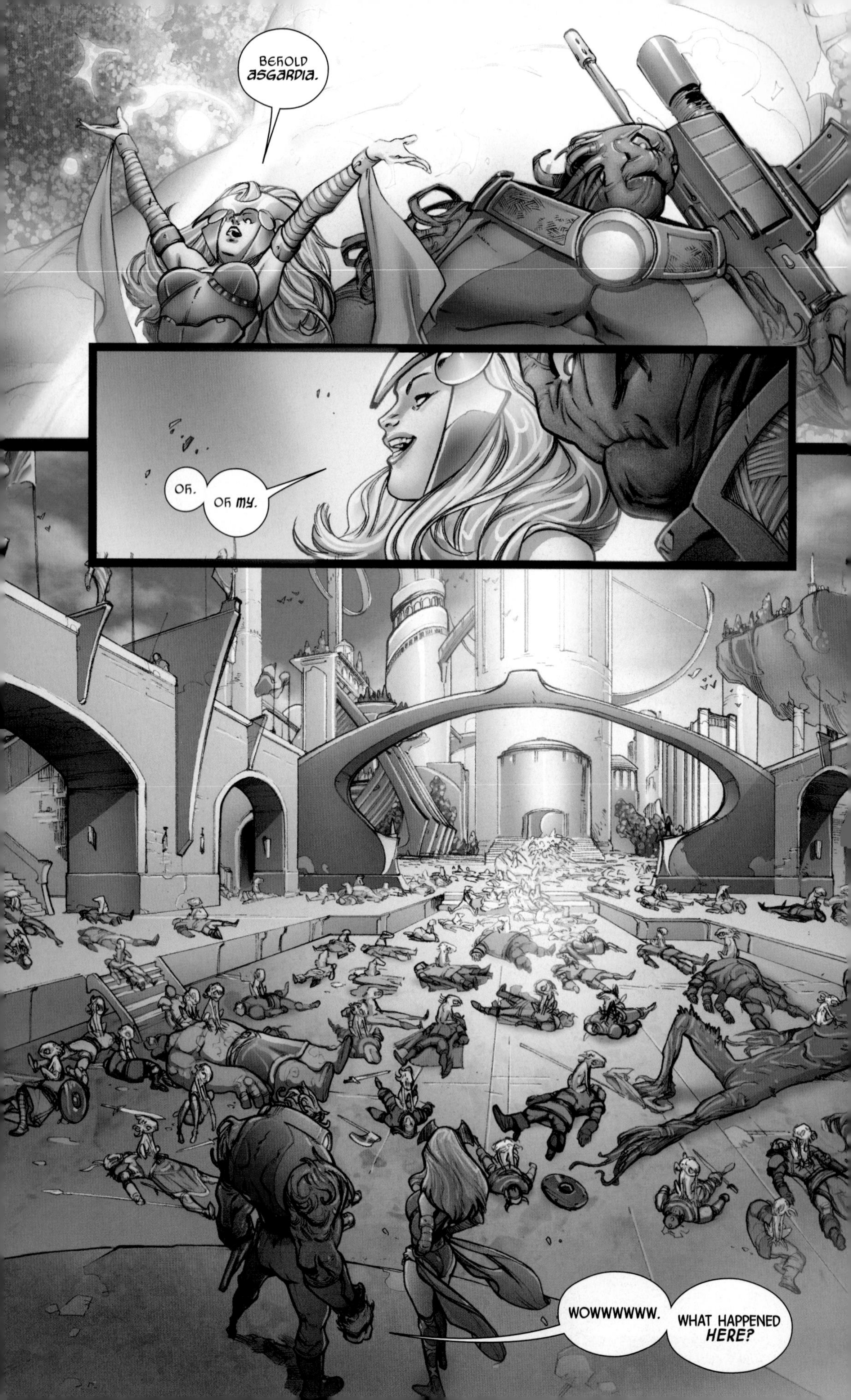
BEHOLD ASGARDIA.
OH.
OH MY.
WOWWWWWW.
WHAT HAPPENED HERE?

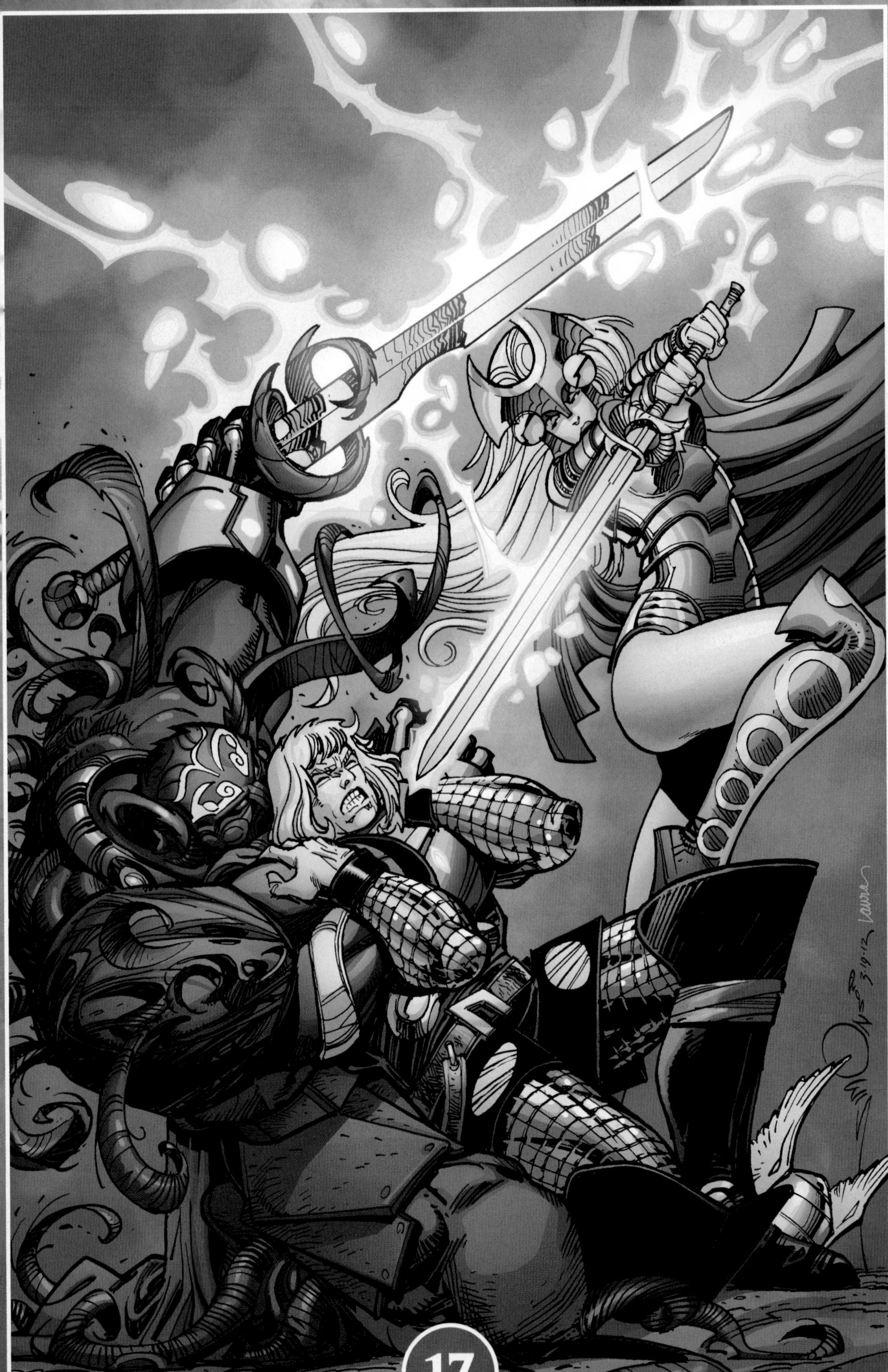
17

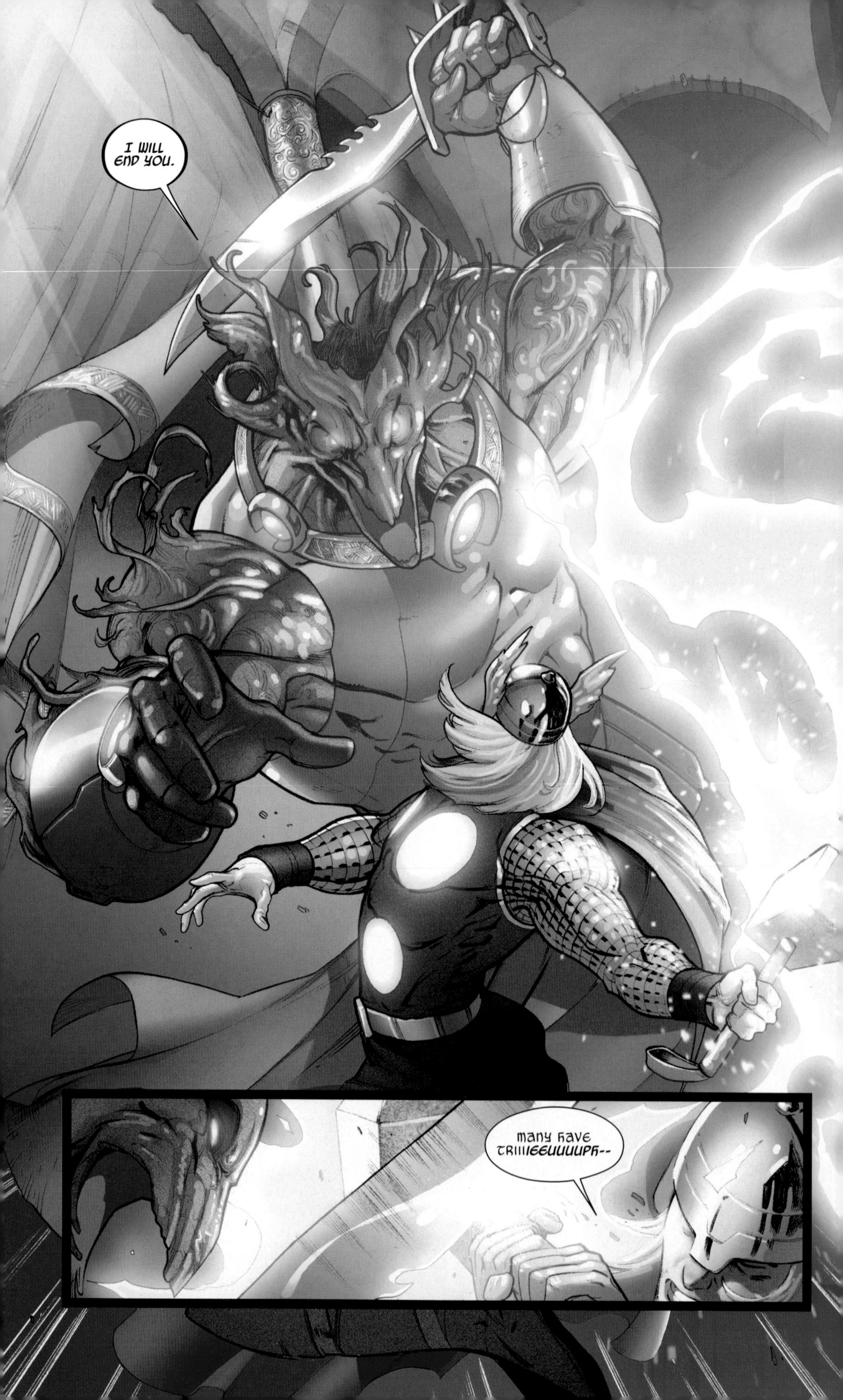
I WILL END YOU.
MANY HAVE TRIIIIEEUUUUPH--

MADAMS ALL-MOTHER...

WE'VE JUST MADE A TERRIBLE *MESS* OF THINGS, I'M AFRAID.

GOOD *FREIDMAR,* ACCEPTING BLAME WHERE THERE IS NONE SOLVES THE PROBLEMS OF NO ONE.

'TIS A PROBLEM FOR ALL THE NINE REALMS, IT WOULD APPEAR.

WELL, ABOUT THAT. THE *REALMS* ARE HOME TO POWERFUL BEINGS AND THOSE BEINGS HAVE POWERFUL DREAMS.

AND STAGGERING *NIGHTMARES.*

THE *SENSITIVES* SNIFFED OUT BY OUR *DIRE MONKS* WERE MEANT TO--

--OH NO--

--NOT AGAIN!

NOT AGAIN, BOY! AWAKE!

"AWAKE WITH YOU!"

WHOA.

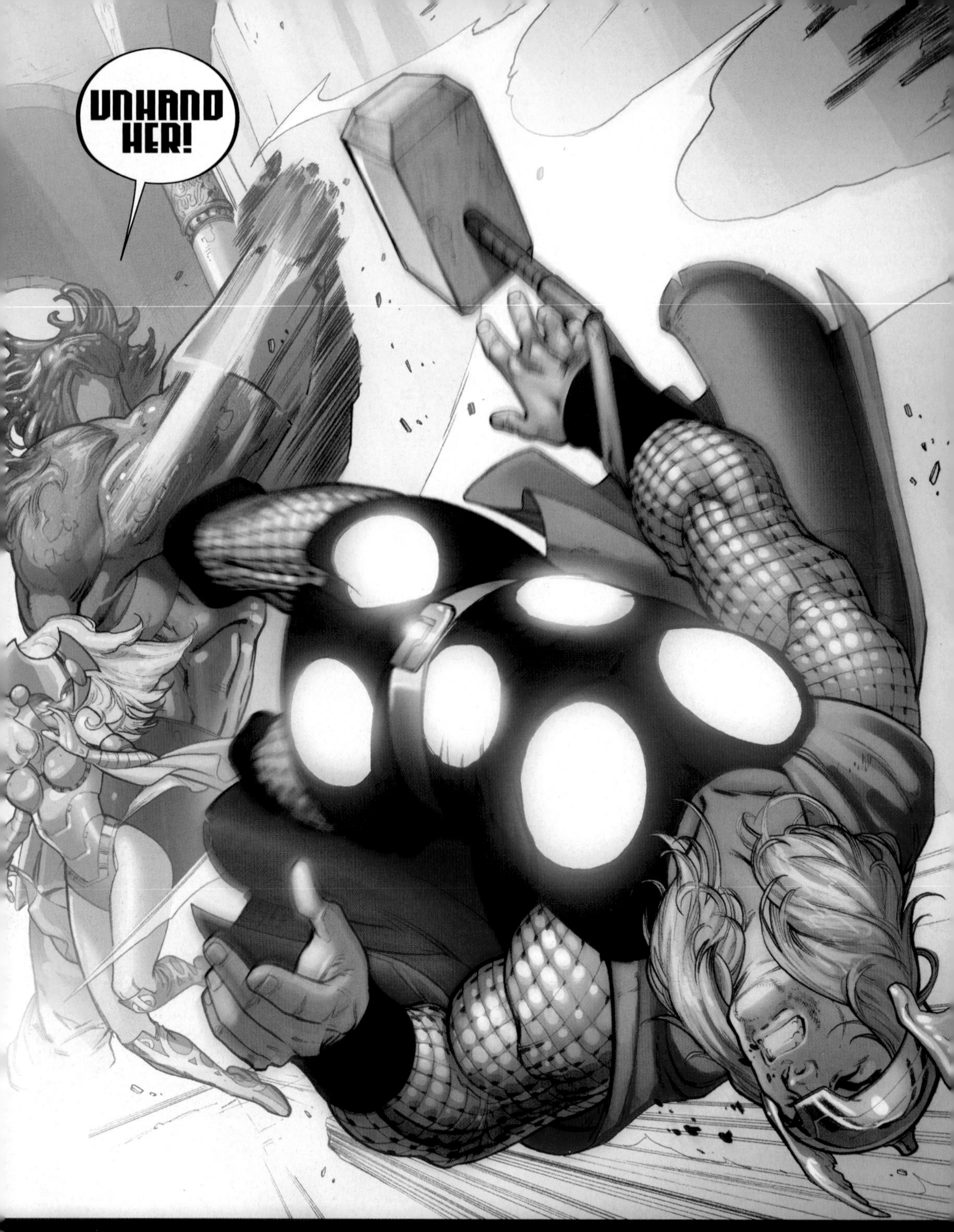
UNHAND HER!

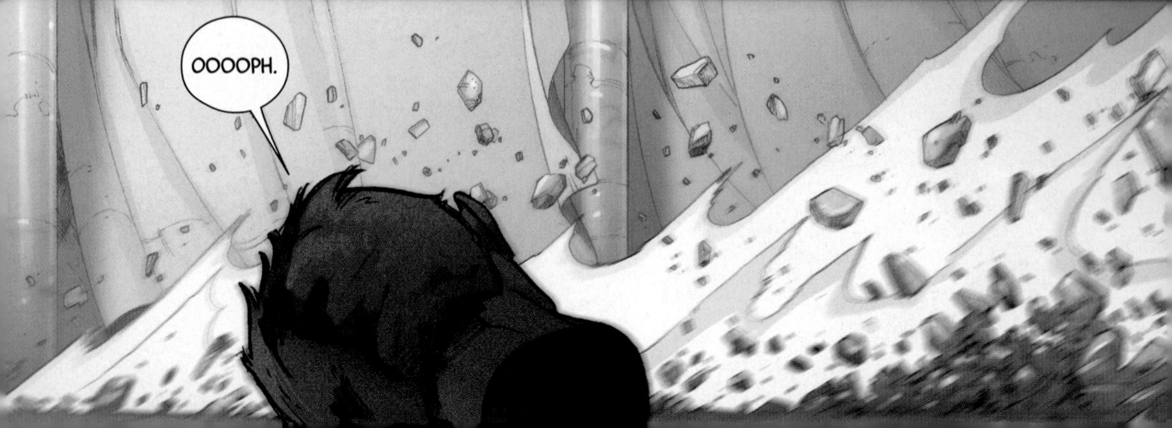
OOOOPH.

"YOU RETURN FROM *NIDAVELLIR* AND THE *MARELOCK* WITH GOOD WORD, WE TRUST."

I DO AT THAT...

THEY WANT A VOICE IN THE PARLIAMENT OF REALMS, THEY WANT A PRESENCE. THEY WANT TO NOT BE *ODIN-BOUND* IN A *CAVE* ANYMORE...

UNLIKE THE THUNDER GOD TO HAVE A *DEBT* HANGING OVER HIS HEAD.

TELL US, THOR--WHAT COULD YOU POSSIBLY OWE THE MARES TO ENSURE PEACE BETWEEN OUR KINDS?

THERE WILL BE PEACE. TO ENSURE IT, THEY GRANTED ME A *BOON.* NOW I'M IN THEIR DEBT.

I...

SHE WASN'T WRONG, THE ENCHANTRESS

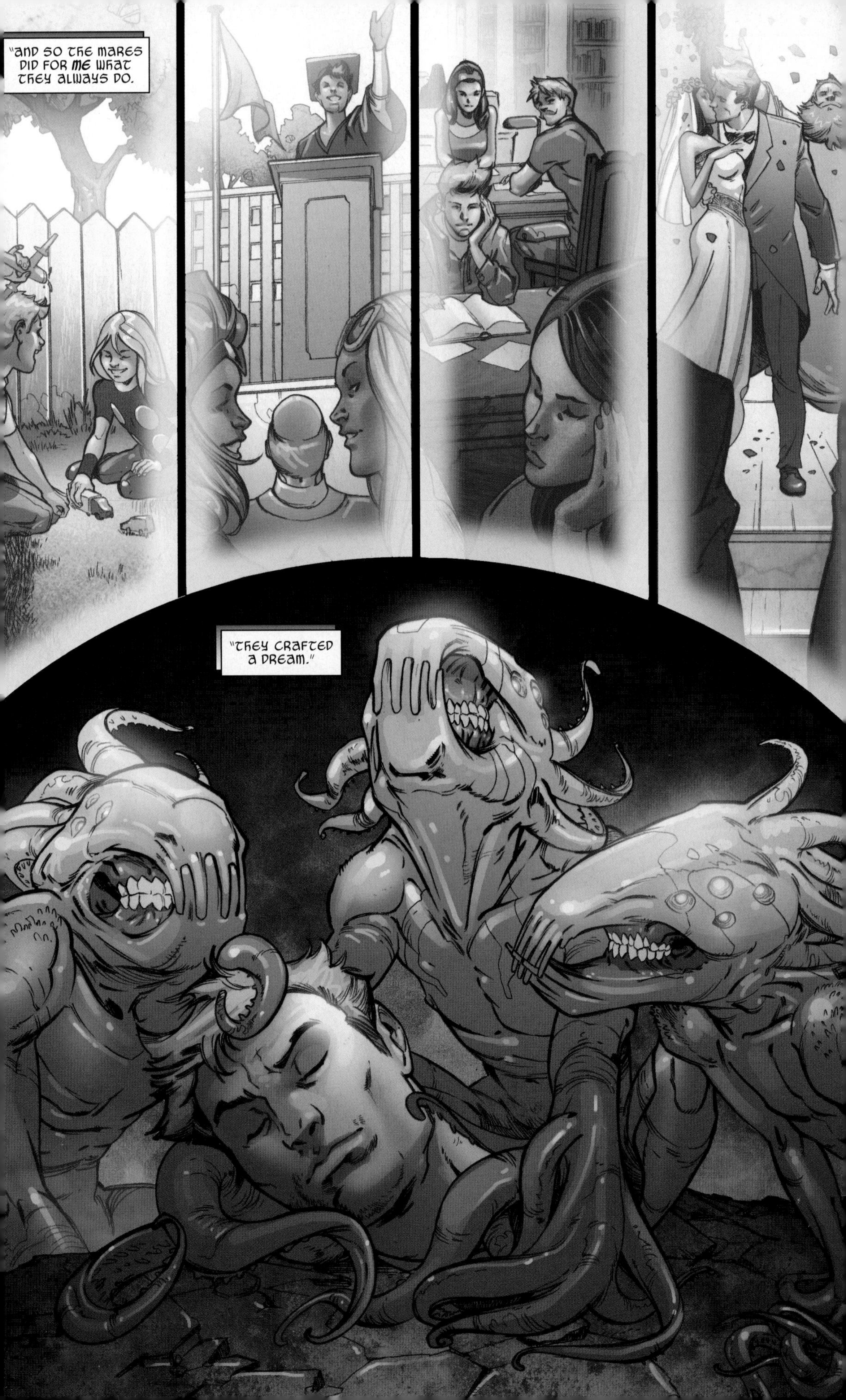
"AND SO THE MARES DID FOR ME WHAT THEY ALWAYS DO.
"THEY CRAFTED A DREAM."

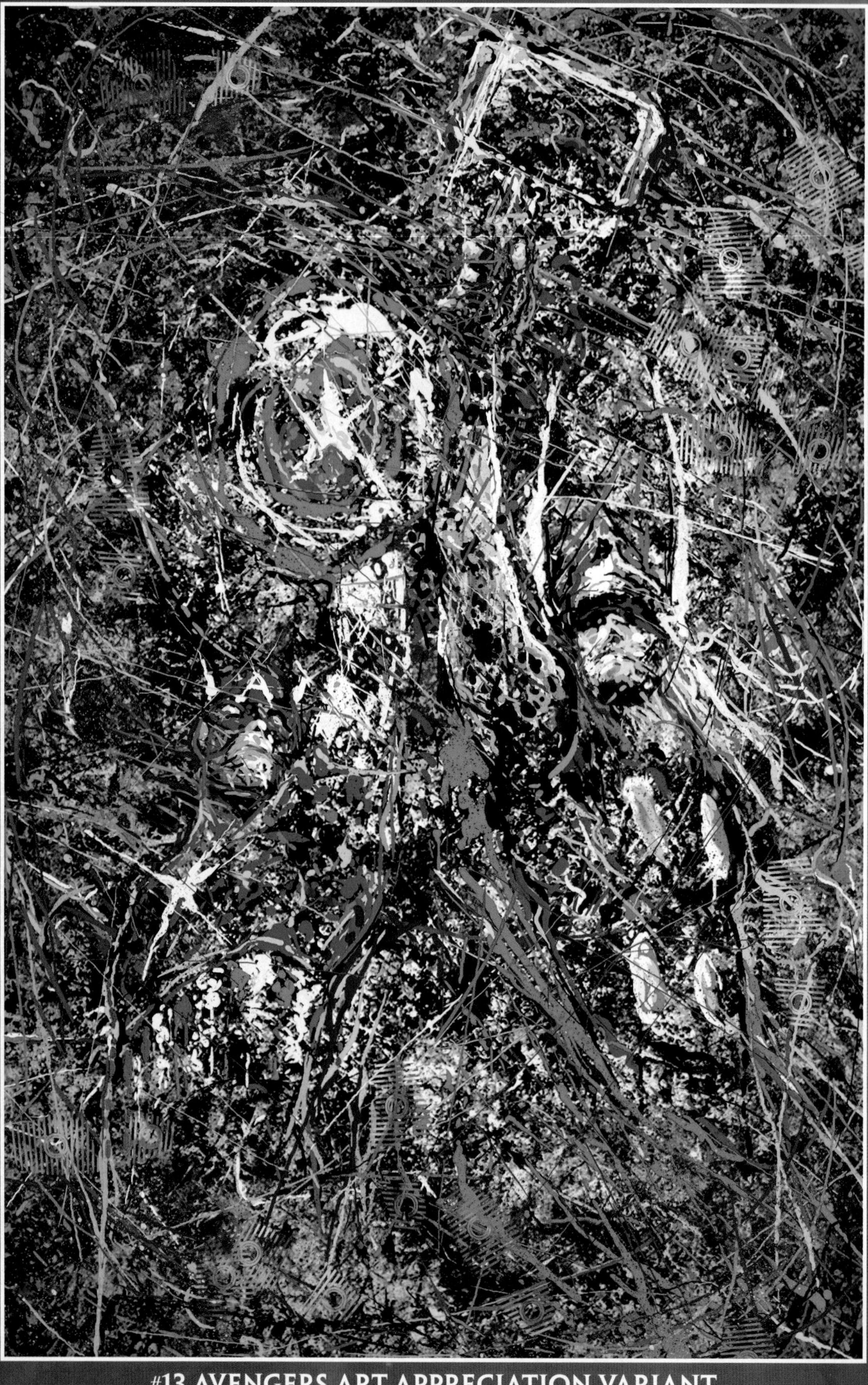

#13 AVENGERS ART APPRECIATION VARIANT
BY RICHARD ISANOVE

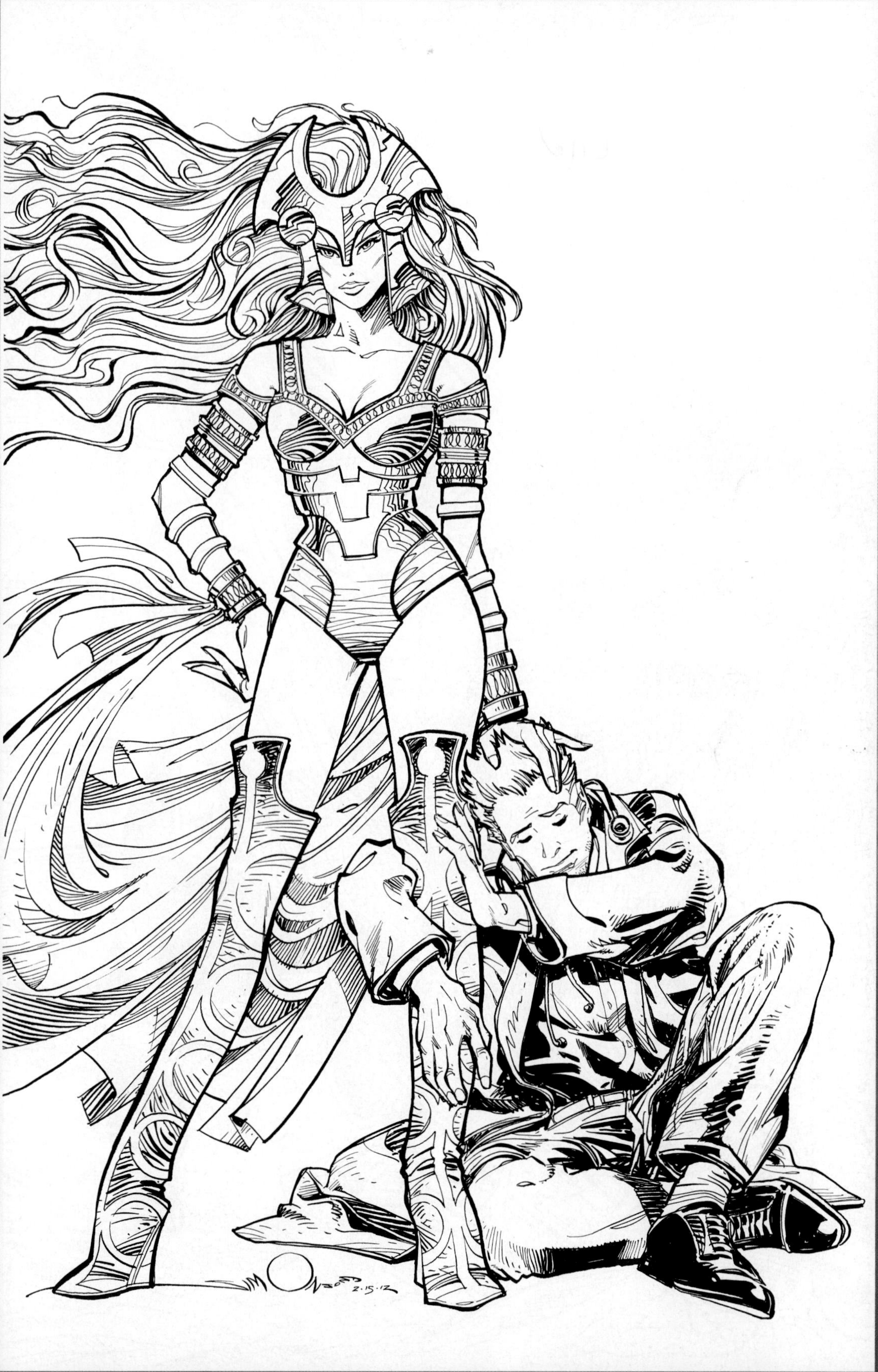

#13 COVER INKS

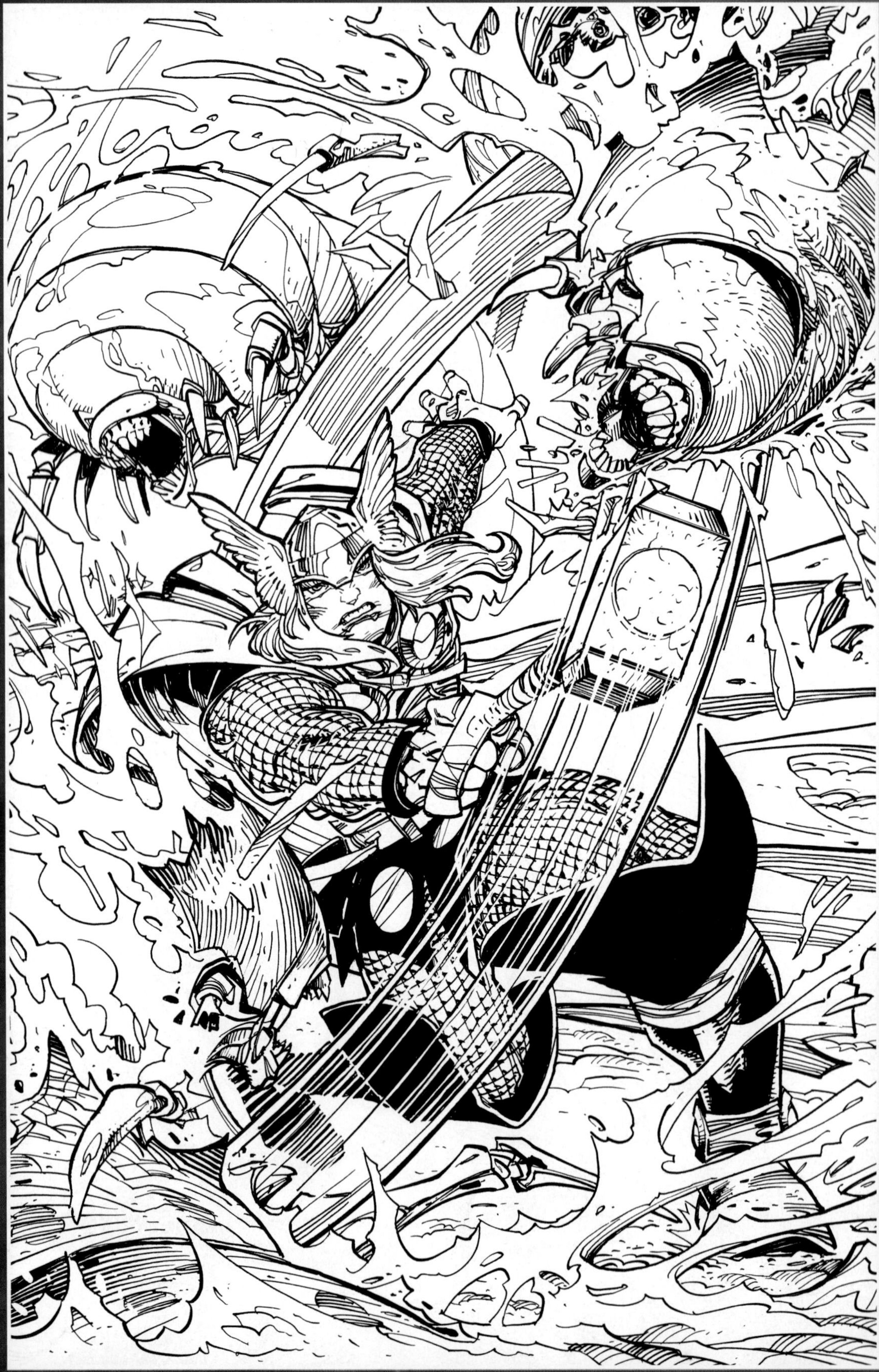

#14 COVER INKS

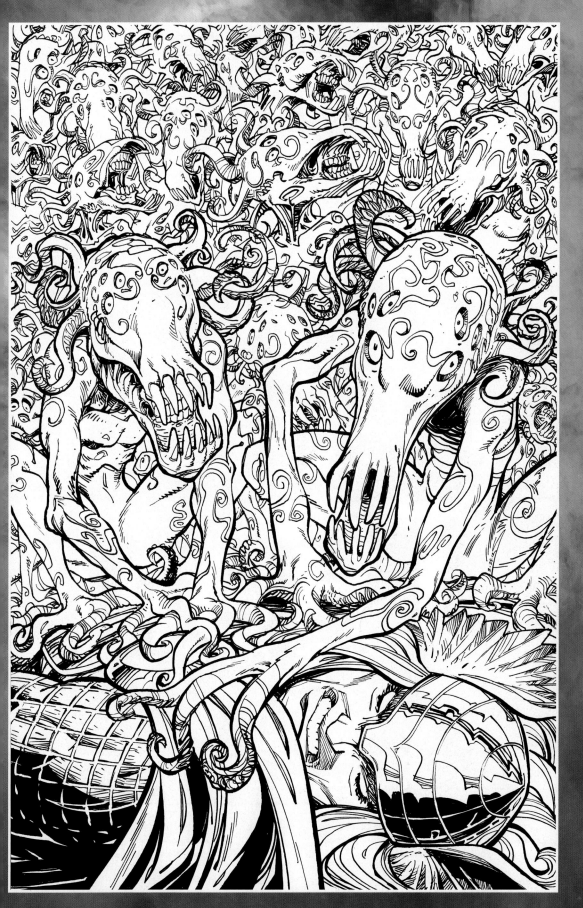

#16 COVER INKS

"IT'S A BEAUTIFUL BOOK TO LOOK AT AND REA ." - *A COMIC*

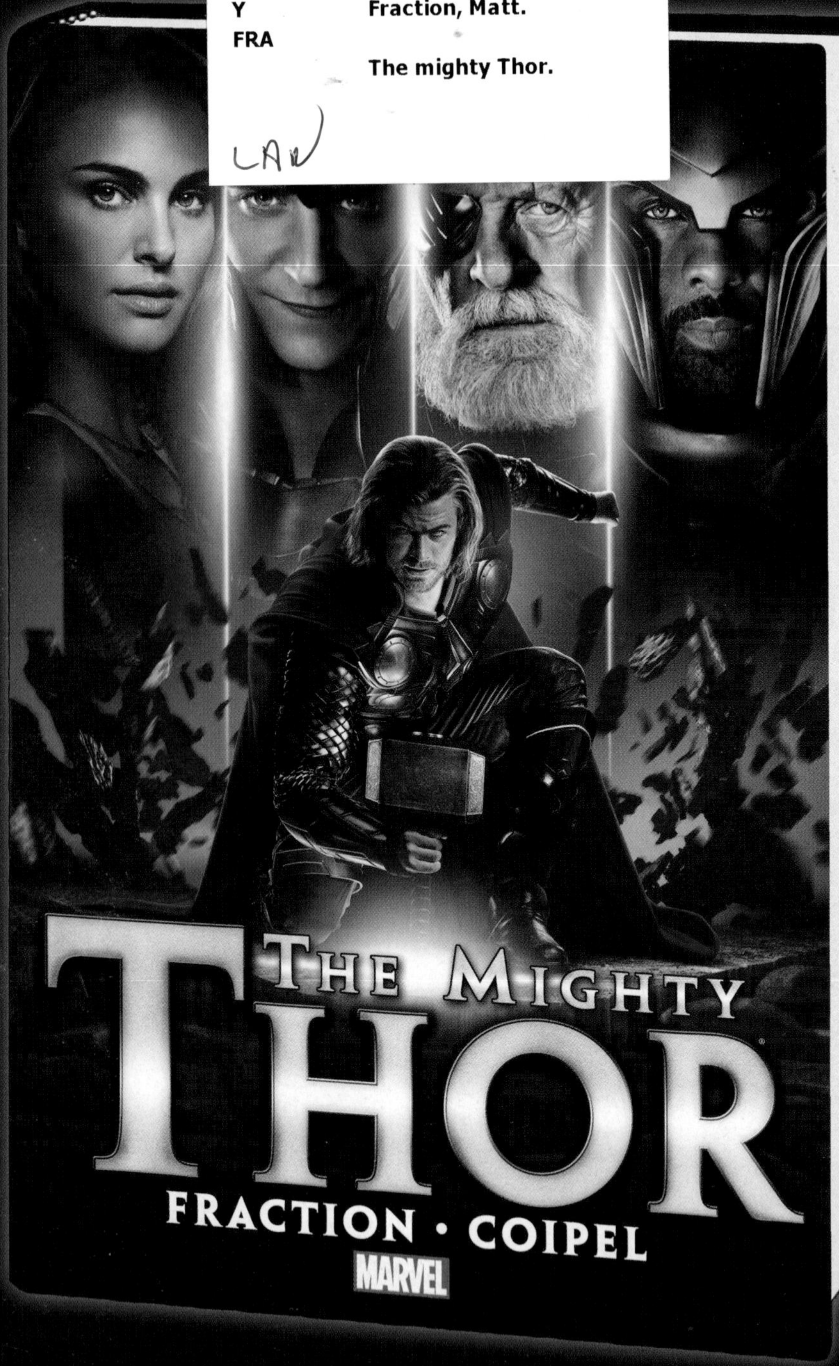
THE MIGHTY
THOR
FRACTION · COIPEL
MARVEL

THE MIGHTY THOR BY MATT FRACTION VOL. 1 PREMIERE HC
978-0-7851-5691-8

ALSO AVAILABLE

THOR BY J. MICHAEL STRACZYNSKI VOL. 1 TPB
978-0-7851-1722-3

THOR BY KIERON GILLEN ULTIMATE CO
978-0-7851-5922-3